Wiggins

Mark Twain
Jackleg Novelist

MARK TWAIN

JACKLEG NOVELIST

MARK TWAIN
JACKLEG NOVELIST

By

ROBERT A. WIGGINS

UNIVERSITY OF WASHINGTON PRESS

SEATTLE 1964

For Lilli, Roberta, and Julie

"*WOULD THE READER* care to know

something about the story which I pulled out?

He has been told many a time

how the born-and-trained novelist works.

Won't he let me round and complete his knowledge

by telling him how the jackleg does it?"

THOSE EXTRAORDINARY TWINS

Preface

A FRIEND to whom I showed the manuscript commented that the angle from which I examine Mark Twain as a novelist is heretical for our time and that my approach will arouse some resistance from the Mark Twain specialists. I did not deliberately set out to defy the Mark Twain fraternity. I thought I would try to make some common-sense judgments about the art of the novel as practiced by Twain without fashionable critical terminology and without the restrictions imposed by a narrow set of critical assumptions.

Perhaps I shall be regarded as ingenuous, even naive, to proceed so simply. In doing so one runs the risk of being accused of reducing rich complexities to obvious oversimplifications. I think it is a risk worth taking. The reverse is just as serious an error. There is a danger in seeing only the many fine things in Twain's fiction, in becoming so partisan that one is not merely blind to his faults but must see virtues where they do not exist.

This book is an attempt to define and assess Mark Twain's achievement as a novelist. The title, taken from Twain's own statement, indicates the central theme. The term *jackleg* in nineteenth-century colloquial usage meant an impostor or incompetent workman. We must make allowance for Twain's customary exaggeration, but when he refers to himself as a jackleg he reflects his uneasiness at being cast in the role of a novelist.

Twain thought a great deal about the craft of fiction, however, and he was not lacking in opinions on the subject. He had a certain mastery of the details that went into the making of a notable prose style, but he also relied upon inspiration and a questionable taste to guide him in areas of his craft where he was unsure. I do not take Twain's term *jackleg* as necessarily one of disparagement. It does serve to suggest that he was an improvisor. He deliberately depended upon "the unconscious" to inspire his pen, rather than craft or "manufacture."

In the first two chapters I have tried to indicate that Twain's highly personal approach to fiction was based in his limited understanding of realism and humor. They were paramount in the fictional method he evolved. In the remaining chapters I have discussed each of his novels, partly to show something of Twain's virtues and limitations, but also to demonstrate how his method operated. In the process the story becomes the chronicle of an artist's not always successful attempt to wrest meaning from his experience, using his art as an instrument through which he might make discoveries he could share with his fellow man.

The aspects of his craft that he knew best were rendering the speech of the common man and recreating the details of a segment of American life well known to him. In the process he delighted his audience with his engaging personality; he was a dazzling performer as the spokesman for the common sense of the people. Unfortunately he did not know to what extent his virtues sprang from his identity with a strong and pervasive American folk tradition. He could not know that his public popularity was in part self-congratulatory, that in Twain the public was approving an image of itself.

Twain's technical equipment, the strategies and devices he developed for handling characters and incidents, were admirably adapted to the materials he knew best. They served him well when he trusted his deepest sympathies and allowed his material to dictate its own form. His difficulties as a novelist developed when he became self-conscious about the novel. His understanding of the structure of a novel was rudimentary, his critical intelligence insufficient. Twain the man tried to adapt to a genteel culture; Twain the artist failed, in part, to understand what this was doing to his art.

It is fruitless to speculate on what might have been Mark Twain's achievement had he had the advantages of a university education. He would not have been Mark Twain. His genius, in-

stead of being liberated further, might have been modified into
that of a minor genteel scribbler. Let us accept what we have—
an artist who discovered an artistic method uniquely his own.
When it worked, it produced a *Huckleberry Finn* or *The Mysterious Stranger*. When it failed, it often produced splendid failures. The rest we can forgive.

A number of friends and colleagues have given suggestions and
comment. James D. Hart read early versions of several chapters.
Caroline Gordon, Celeste Wright, William Van O'Connor, and
Malcolm Cowley all read the manuscript and offered good advice. I am more grateful to them than I can adequately express.
To them must go credit for this being a better book than they
first saw.

Contents

xi

MARK TWAIN

JACKLEG NOVELIST

I

"Fellow-teachers of the Great Public"

On the night of December 7, 1877, Mark Twain endured what was probably the most shattering experience of his literary career. It was on the occasion of the famous Whittier birthday dinner.

Twain's biographers, critics, and contemporaries have often referred to the incident. Their usual attitude has been one of sympathy with Twain, regarding it as an illustration of the gulf separating the New England mind and the breezy, free-wheeling western personality. Others have seen it as an example of Twain's hypersensitive nature, and one of the few occasions on which he misjudged the temper of his audience. What discredit now attaches to the affair is charged to the stuffy Boston audience.

There is more to the incident, however, than one of life's most embarrassing moments. It was traumatic for Twain's literary psyche. The full story reveals his deep-seated insecurity as a writer and is especially relevant to his career as a novelist. Years later, in 1892, he would refer to himself as a jackleg, and he insisted in 1889 that he wrote for the masses rather than the classes. One wonders to what extent this attitude may have been a rationalization, for there was another side to Twain that earlier had aspired to critical recognition, that wanted the approval of the Boston literati.

Bret Harte understood this aspect of Twain. He had known Twain well in the San Francisco days, and saw him once again upon moving to the East to be received as an equal by the *Atlantic Monthly* group. William Dean Howells in *My Mark Twain* tells of a luncheon in the winter of 1871 with Twain, Harte, T. B. Aldrich, and James T. Field. He remembered "Bret Harte's fleering dramatization of Clemens's mental attitude toward a symposium of Boston illuminates. 'Why, fellows,' he spluttered, 'this is the dream of Mark's life.' " [1]

There is also no doubt of Twain's enormous pleasure at making his debut in the *Atlantic* in 1874. His biographer, Albert Bigelow Paine, quotes Joseph Twichell's remembrance of Twain's "mingled astonishment and triumph" when invited to contribute. Several pieces were rejected as unsuitable before "A True Story," one that Twain himself characterized as "rather out of my line," was accepted. The next three years Twain's magazine appearance was exclusively in the *Atlantic*, though Howells makes clear that he could have commanded much higher prices elsewhere. The chief of these contributions was "Old Times on the Mississippi."

Howells also comments upon the slowness of literary Boston to recognize Twain's gifts, in spite of—perhaps because of—his great popularity with his mass audience at home and his acceptance in polite circles abroad. "I went with him to see Longfellow, but I do not think Longfellow made much of him, and Lowell made less. He stopped as if with the long Semitic curve of Clemens's nose, which in the indulgence of his passion for finding every one more or less a Jew he pronounced unmistakably racial." The only exceptions were Charles Eliot Norton and Professor Francis J. Child.

> I cannot say just why Clemens seemed not to hit the favor of our community of scribes and scholars, as Bret Harte had done, when he came on from California, and swept them before him, disrupting their dinners and delaying their lunches with impunity; but it is certain he did not, and I had better say so.[2]

Twain must have felt that his slow climb to favor had progressed in his three years of association with the *Atlantic*. He had been invited a number of times to lunches and dinners given by the editors and publishers. His friendship with Howells grew, and *Tom Sawyer* had added to his stature. But if he felt any security in Brahmin company, it must have been shaken on the night of the Whittier dinner.

Twain had been asked to speak, and he went about making his

preparations more elaborately than was his custom. He was un-
usually secretive. Not even his wife knew what he was up to; she
undoubtedly would have disapproved of the nature of his speech.
With secret delight Twain must have looked forward to the reception of his speech as the high spot of the evening. It was. But
not in the terms he anticipated.

The dinner was held in the Brunswick Hotel. Mark Twain
found his place at the outside of one leg of the horseshoe banquet
table near his friend James R. Osgood, the bookseller and pub-
lisher. He was one of about fifty guests in the audience. At the
head of the U-shaped table sat the chief guests. On the left were
Longfellow and Emerson. Then next came Whittier, the guest of
honor, with Mr. Houghton, the new owner of the *Atlantic* and
host for the evening, beside him. Howells, the toastmaster, was
next, with Doctor Holmes completing the table on the right.

The company worked through a lengthy menu, and Mr.
Houghton did not rap for attention until after ten o'clock. At this
time the company was augmented by additional guests, who had
not attended the dinner, but came for the speeches. The prelimi-
naries took some time. There were letters to be read from dig-
nitaries who could not attend. Finally Howells introduced Twain.
It was a full and admiring introduction, but the part that stuck
in the mind, in view of what followed, was Howells' attribution
of genteel qualities to Twain's humor. His words now take on an
ironic cast. Twain was "a humorist who never left you hanging
your head for having enjoyed his joke." Then in the words that
Howells used years later in remembering the scene, "The amazing
mistake, the bewildering blunder, the cruel catastrophe was upon
us." [3]

Twain rose to speak. His bushy shock of graying auburn hair
made him seem taller than he was. In his customary drawl he began to spin a yarn about the time in the West when he had
achieved some local fame as a writer. He once claimed hospitality
of a lone miner by introducing himself as Mark Twain. He got
a cool reception from the miner, who said that Twain was "the
fourth littery man that has been here in twenty-four hours—I'm
going to move." Then in the comic tones of the miner Twain
drawled his story of how the night before he had been visited by

three men introducing themselves as Mr. Longfellow, Mr. Emerson, and Mr. Oliver Wendell Holmes. The miner goes on to describe the curious behavior of the three as they salted their conversation and card game with appropriate quotations. Twain explained that the three men were impostors, and the miner then asks, "Ah! impostors, were they? Are you?"

Twain, of course, had in his imagination pictured those at the head table convulsed with laughter, but only silence greeted his fanciful speech. Longfellow stared straight ahead. Emerson, lost in a fog, had not heard a word. Holmes busied himself through the tale by writing on his menu. Poor Howells stared at his plate in embarrassment. The rest of the company closed ranks in silence against the outsider mocking the tribal totems.

The fiasco, as others have suggested, can be seen as a kind of literary-social allegory. The vernacular style of the masses was challenging the literary dominance of the genteel tradition. The literary high priests of Brahmin culture could respond in no other way than they did—with the conventions of "well-bred," icy good manners. Twain was not consciously making a gesture; he was only being himself.

Any other writer confident of his worth, secure in his belief in his talent, would have offered apology for any unintended offense taken, and let the matter drop. But not Twain. He suffered. There is a clue at the end of the tale in the miner's words, "Ah! impostors, were they? Are you?" Twain presents himself as the butt of a joke. The audience did not laugh. Twain must have felt his insecurity regarding his literary credentials well-founded, his misgivings at being in this "grave and stately company" perhaps confirmed.

Howells tells how stricken Twain was after the dinner, and Twain's subsequent behavior testifies to the enormity of his offense in his own mind. He wrote Howells:

> My sense of disgrace does not abate. It grows. . . .
> I feel that my misfortune has injured me all over the country; therefore it will be best that I retire from before the public at present. It will hurt the *Atlantic* for me to appear in its pages now. . . .
> It seems as if I must have been insane when I wrote that speech and saw no harm in it, no disrespect toward those men whom I

reverenced so much. And what shame I brought upon *you*, after what you said in introducing me! It burns me like fire to think of it.

The whole matter is a dreadful subject. Let me drop it here—at least on paper.

Penitently yours,
Mark [4]

A few days afterward Twain wrote identical abjectly apologetic letters to Longfellow, Holmes, and Emerson.

Gentlemen: I come before you now, with the mien and posture of the guilty—not to excuse, gloss, or extenuate, but only to offer my repentance. . . . But I do not ask you to forgive what I did that night, for it is not forgivable; I simply had it at heart to ask you to believe that I am only heedlessly a savage, not premeditatedly; & I am under as severe punishment as even you could adjudge to me if you were required to appoint my penalty. I do not ask you to say one word in answer to this; it is not needful, & would of course be distasteful & difficult. I beg you to consider that in letting me unbosom myself you will do me an act of grace that will be sufficient in itself.[5]

Even a Brahmin could not ask for more. Longfellow, in replying, blamed the newspapers for finding disrespect in the speech.

A bit of humor at a dinner-table talk is one thing; a report of it in the morning papers is another. One needs the lamplight and the scenery. These failing, what was meant in jest assumes a serious aspect.

I do not believe that anybody was much hurt. Certainly I was not, and Holmes tells me he was not. So I think you may dismiss the matter from your mind, without further remorse.[6]

Holmes also reassured Twain in well-bred tones.

It never occurred to me for a moment to take offense, or to feel wounded by your playful use of my name. I have heard some mild questioning as to whether, even in fun, it was good taste to associate the names of the authors with the absurdly unlike personalities attributed to them, but it seems to be an open question. Two of my friends, gentlemen of education and the highest social standing, were infinitely amused by your speech, and stoutly defended it against the charge of impropriety. More than this, one of the cleverest and best-known ladies we have among us was highly delighted with it.[7]

Both gentlemen politely indicate that they were not offended. But the fact remains that if either of them had so much as smiled during the speech there would have been no incident. Ellen Emerson, writing for her father and the family, was a bit more candid in concluding her forgiving letter. "I think you can see just *how* bad, and how little bad, it was as far as we are concerned, and this lovely heartbreaking letter makes up for our disappointment in our much-liked author, and restores our former feeling about him." [8]

In another letter to Howells, Twain said, "I haven't done a stroke of work since the Atlantic dinner; have only moped around." [9] There is no doubt that the affair made a profound impression upon Twain. It did not change him outwardly, but it certainly contributed to his artistic insecurity. For years he remained apologetic about appearing outside his role of humorist-satirist.

The sequel to the Whittier dinner occurred exactly two years later in two events. In November, 1879, Twain traveled to Chicago for the reunion of the Army of the Tennessee with General Grant as the featured guest. Twain's toast to the babies at the banquet was the triumph of the evening. It was fancifully built around the image of Grant as a baby with toe in mouth. It was the sort of thing he had tried two years before, and this time in less constrained company it was a success.

A month later he attended an *Atlantic* breakfast given for Holmes. It was the first time he had been in this company since the Whittier dinner. In accepting the invitation Twain wrote to Howells.

> If anybody talks, there, I shall claim the right to say a word myself, and be heard among the very *earliest*—else it would be confoundedly awkward for me—and for the rest, too. But you may read what I say, beforehand, and strike out whatever you choose.
>
> Of course I thought it wisest not to be there at all; but Warner took the opposite view, and most strenuously. [10]

Substantially the same company gathered for Holmes's birthday that had been present for the Whittier dinner. Longfellow, Emerson, and Whittier were there, as well as some who were not at the former event—Francis Parkman and Harriet Beecher Stowe, for example. Howells introduced Twain by saying, "We will now listen to a few words of truth and soberness from Mark Twain." Twain told how he first made Holmes's acquaintance when he acknowledged an innocent bit of plagiarism and how Holmes graciously replied. It was a witty and graceful compliment. In concluding Twain unobtrusively asserted his right to sit in this company.

> I have met Dr. Holmes many times since; and he lately said— However, I am wandering wildly away from the one thing which I got to my feet to do; that is, to make my compliments to you, my fellow-teachers of the great public, and likewise to say I am right glad to see that Dr. Holmes is still in his prime and full of generous life, and as age is not determined by years but by trouble, and by infirmities of mind and body, I hope it may be a very long time yet before any can truthfully say, "He is growing old."

Twain may still have felt uneasy in Brahmin company; he may have felt himself to be a maverick and a jackleg. But there is no doubt that he also felt committed firmly to the profession of letters and shared with the company a bond; of whatever sort, they were all "fellow-teachers of the great public."

No mortal can escape the consequences of his decisions. Twain was no exception. Two choices he made early as a writer played a large part in setting the limits of his style as well as in forming the basis for one of the notable styles in American letters. The first choice was to portray life in his fiction as truthfully as he could. It accounts for his developing a realistic style that always depicts his subject in concrete, specific, economical, and exact prose, constantly tested against his own experience and what he believed to be true and real. The second choice, that of humor as his most characteristic mode of expression, brought with it a number of attendant consequences. The longer he persisted in following his success as a humorist, the more rigidly be became committed to a serious limitation of his range of expression and the more fixed became his relation to his audience. Twain later seems to have realized this result, chafed under its restriction, and explored the possibilities of achievement within the confines of humor, of expanding these limits as well as freeing himself of them.

Twain's option for literary realism placed him within what would prove to be the main stream of prose fiction as it developed in the latter part of the nineteenth century. Indeed, more than most of his contemporaries Twain even anticipates the literary naturalists, who were later to follow upon the realists of the nineteenth century. So far as his intention—not necessarily his performance—was concerned, it seems certain that he deliberately wielded the tools of his craft in the interests of greater realism in fiction.

He was perhaps aware of the occasional disparity between his intention and performance when he wrote in "How To Tell A Story": "I do not claim that I can tell a story as it ought to be told. I only claim to know how a story ought to be told." He was writing specifically about the art of oral narration, but he could have included the novel form with equal truth. He thought he knew how fiction should be written, but he was not always certain of the results of his labor. Thus the accusation of unconsciousness can be leveled not at his intention, but rather at his deliberately cultivated method of treatment—his dependence upon inspiration to provide a suitable form for his material.

> When there is reasonable doubt in the case of a ms. of yours, your instinct detects it every time, and you ought to lay that piece of paper away, until some future time, when the right way to treat the subject shall have come to you from that mill whose helpful machinery never stands idle—unconscious cerebration. But nothing is really lost; there is always a right way to treat a subject, and the U. C. will find it if you give it time; which time will not be short of two years and will often be nine. I am speaking from personal experience.[11]

This advice was given years after the production of his novels and is colored by his mechanistic philosophy, but it does indicate something of Twain's approach toward creating his novels. But in fairness it is not true to say that "unconscious cerebration" supplied the material and form; even in those works where the system seems to have operated, Twain was more in control of his material than his statement would indicate.

By the time Twain began to write novels, his style was substantially formed; when he approached the task of beginning a work, his conception of the story to follow was conditioned by habits developed in his apprentice writing. Certainly, no author is entirely aware of all such factors operating in his work. But neither was Twain entirely unaware of them. This awareness of the elements of his craft seems to have grown in direct proportion as he moved from theoretical consideration of larger matters toward more specific and concrete concern with detail. He talked a great deal about the technique of humor, but actually Mark Twain had only a limited conception of this most central element of his art. And in planning a novel, he was conscious of the fact that he could not entirely account for the creative process in which he was involved. But in the smaller elements of his art—the incident, the paragraph, the sentence, the word—Twain was a self-conscious, skilled craftsman, even to a more profound extent than most of his critics have admitted.

The second choice he made—his commitment to humor—established a relationship between Twain and his audience: on one side he knew his audience well, but on the other his audience knew him primarily as a "phunny phellow." His own background of experience, because it was so comprehensive, had many points of contact with that of the average American of his day. He had lived on the level of his audience, and from actual acquaintance he knew that common man—provincial, socially and intellectually limited, narrowed in experience by the conditions of a recent pioneer past. But Twain was also removed from this audience in that he had been in contact with other social and intellectual levels of society, where his journalistic training served him as a close observer of people. Twain also came in contact with his audience in a way that few other novelists had been privileged to do. The people he wrote for were, for the most part, the same to whom he lectured. He studied the audience carefully, for his success as a lecturer depended greatly upon his ability to judge his audience and to sense reactions almost before they occurred. Only rarely did he seriously miscalculate his audience.

This need to please his audience imposed certain obligations. His letters show his dislike for the lecture circuit, his repeated resolutions not to accept offers, and his disgust for his role as a buffoon. Twain's antipathy seems to have been directed not against appearing before an audience, but rather at the inconveniences in traveling the lecture circuit. But he had to lecture for money until his books assured enough income for him to abandon the lecture platform.

Nor would he write a book unless there was money in it. We may be tempted to call this attitude toward his profession crass and commercial, but it was one he shared with others. A more charitable view would say he took a professional attitude toward his writing. Howells himself wanted the highest returns he could get for his literary labors, and Twain's neighbors at Nook Farm felt the same way. Twain would have been the first to laugh at the notion that he was an artist creating works without regard for their market. He was a public entertainer, and he accepted the obligation imposed. He was honest; he would not knowingly trade a shoddy product. For value received he contracted to produce an equivalent amount of entertainment, even if sometimes he had to strain his humor and pad his wordage with borrowed material to meet his deadline.

Continued exploitation of his early successes required further exploration of the possibilities of humor. But being committed in this way seems not to have troubled Twain at first. He thought he could write almost anything so long as he made it entertaining. That was his obligation, and he entertained most easily by making people laugh. Rarely does Twain fail to entertain. Children, the severest critics of this elemental requisite, are almost never disappointed in Twain's stories. I do not mean to imply puerility on Twain's part, but only to say that he had mastered this aspect of the art of fiction so often forgotten by more sophisticated writers.

Although his audience limited Twain by forcing him to avoid such a subject as sex, the fact hardly seems sufficient reason to justify the wailing some critics have done on this subject. Since he could not treat sex realistically, Twain for the most part left the subject alone. Other aspects of man's animal nature he did describe, and again some critics, unhappy at Twain's silence concerning sex, are offended by his grossness in finding *mal de mer* and overripe corpses subjects for laughter. A just sense of proportion would find greater cause for concern in the fact that Twain's confined notion of humor seriously limited his treatment of many other of mankind's major concerns. Man's relation to art, politics, and thought, for example, are handled generally only as they admit of humorous treatment. Of course, Twain did often make pungent comments upon these subjects, but always from the point of view of the humorist and satirist.

In *Tom Sawyer*, for example, numerous inherently serious subjects are raised and dwelt upon at varying length: drunkenness, lying, stealing, learning, injustice, brutality, and irreverence, among many others, are dealt with in the different adventures, but only as they permit high jinks, fun, and adventure in the lives of the boys. And even the grimmer episodes of grave robbing, murder, and starving in the cave apparently left no lasting impression upon the characters of the participants. One receives, after all, a distorted picture of the life of the village. The details may be realistically presented so far as verisimilitude is concerned, but they are seen from the limited viewpoint of boyish hilarity almost unrelieved by any seriousness. The sequel, *Huckleberry Finn*, allows a much better balance between humor and seriousness of purpose.

Mark Twain was temperamentally unable to deal subtly with characters; he did not have the background, training, or inclination for detailed analysis of complex character in fiction. He could handle characters only by ignoring their complexity and reducing their problems to elemental components. But this limitation is also his strength. In the creation of fictional character he is at his best in describing the occupations and concerns of relatively primitive human beings illustrating certain elemental aspects of mankind common to all men. By doing so Twain removes the facade of sophistication and "sivilization" from men and shows them as they really are, at their worst as well as their best. Huck Finn is his greatest achievement in the creation of such character, for within this urchin occurs the elemental moral struggle between good and evil that confronts all mankind. Even the lowest slave or ragamuffin is worthy of the dignity of manhood when he voluntarily strips himself naked of pride and pretension and dons the moral robes that are the proper raiment of humanity.

All his life Twain exhibited the symptoms of a "born reformer," but he never consciously grasped the essentially moral basis of his literary efforts. He mocked and railed, he berated and laughed at mankind's foibles. He was disgusted at man's puniness and conceit; he scathingly attacked man for not realizing his rational potential. Yet the necessity for man to assume moral responsibility was a significant concept of Twain's art. In *Huckleberry Finn* he achieved a coherent statement thus informed, but it is doubtful that Twain was conscious of the importance of this moral issue for his work. Individual morality was so inherently a part of the subject that he could not disentangle it, objectively analyze it, and subsequently regard it as a relevant assumption underlying his best style and most significant subject. His conscious effort was rather toward robbing mankind of morality in the mistaken object of destroying the "Moral Sense." This was the most vulnerable area of Twain's thinking, for when the sum of his position is cast, he is found to be a village freethinker who ultimately denied the most vital element of his art.

That Twain could deal only with relatively simple characters and situations is not to his discredit. To some extent he was aware of his limitations, and in this connection his often quoted statement that he did not choose to appeal to the cultivated classes bears repeating here: "I was not equipped for it, either by native gifts or training. And I never had any ambition in that direction but always hunted for bigger game—the masses." [12] Twain directs his novels to the same primitive, mythic mind of the common man that he portrays. He faithfully depicts his limitations, but he also pictures him at his best as a creature of common sense. Huck is Twain's greatest fictional creation of this sort. Twain, himself nurtured in a primitive background, is the spokesman of the common-sense point of view, and his best fiction consequently is rooted firmly in common-sense morality.

Although Twain occasionally drew upon oddities and freaks, his most characteristic concern was with ordinary, representative individuals. This aspect of Twain's art prompted Howells to observe that

> He portrays and interprets real types, not only with exquisite appreciation and sympathy, but with a force and truth of drawing that makes them permanent. . . . But the innumerable charac-

ters sketched by Mark Twain are actualities, however caricatures —and, usually, they are not so very much caricatured.[13]

It would seem to be a deliberate concern if we may accept Twain's words that instead of the cultivated classes he rather tried to appeal to the masses. Indeed, Bernard DeVoto said, "There can be no doubt that Mark's deliberate effort was to explore the mentality of the common man." [14]

Twain characteristically delineated the common man, but the aspect that concerns Twain and most significantly informs his creation is the common man's identification with the folk. I refer to this folk mind as essentially primitive to emphasize an aspect of it most dominant in Twain's fiction. J. H. Randall speaks of such a mind as follows:

This "primitive mentality," so called because it can now be observed at its purest among the most backward of present-day tribes, was deeply impressed upon the beliefs of the Middle Ages . . . in those beliefs that go back to that time, modern man finds himself most akin to the primitive savage because farthest from the skeptical testing of the scientist. The universal characteristics of such a frame of mind, whether it be found in the South Seas or in the Middle Ages or in the modern backwoods farmer, are abundance of belief and explanation for every event that makes an impression, confident certainty of the truth of these beliefs, and intense dislike of calling these fanciful beliefs into question or subjecting them to any testing. In short, such a mind "understands" the meaning of all things but possesses exact knowledge about only those details of daily technique where error would spell disaster.[15]

This type of mind likes to regard itself as guided by common sense; indeed, it tends to regard common sense as the special province of the folk. In the United States today, such minds are relatively rare, found only in culturally isolated areas. But in Twain's youth such a cast of mind was common in the South, bolstered largely by the vast primitive slave population. In addition, it was spread throughout the advancing frontier wherever the Pike County man chose to move. Twain, who had absorbed more of his culture from the Negro than he was aware, dealt most often with this folk mind in his fiction. It was the mind he knew best and one which he most convincingly delineated. Virtually all of his fiction, whatever the setting, affords abundant examples. But when he examined the folk mind in the setting he knew best, he produced his most rewarding work.

Socially and economically Twain traveled a long way from his folk origins, but intellectually he never entirely left the village. A good bit of Hannibal, Missouri, remained in the elderly Sage of Stormfield. But as a writer he always insisted that his characters and prose were in the service of truth; he strove to present what was true and real in his books. Much of his difficulty sprang from his limited notion of what constitutes truth and reality as translated to the pages of a novel. If he meant by truth that his novels honestly reflected his opinion, one may say he achieved truth. It is probable that Twain had no more than this notion in mind. He believed that he had told the truth realistically, and the reader could take it or leave it. Truth in this sense meant no more than the honest expression of his convictions.

A more sophisticated intelligence conceives of truth in other ways. The artistic truth of a novel derives from the unity of integrated parts. One asks whether the values within the novel are arranged in a coherent scheme. In this sense truth is not opposed to moral falsity; it is not so much a moral as an aesthetic judgment. This artistic truth, or thematic coherence, Twain achieved most significantly in his early novels—*Tom Sawyer* and *Huckleberry Finn*. It is a major criterion by which we judge a work of art, but it is not the only one. Among other things we also judge the relative importance or triviality of the values asserted within a work, and almost universally we accord the highest places to ethical and metaphysical values; it is in this sense that the truth of a novel involves moral judgment. Thus, in addition to having a greater degree of artistic unity than the other novels, *Huckleberry Finn* also rests upon a profounder basis in moral values. In his later works, because of conflicting assumptions and the patent error of his conscious belief, Twain could not achieve either consistent thematic coherence or convincing moral statement. We may regret this fact, but we must deal with his achievement as we find it. Even the least charitable view can find cheer in thinking that, in spite of his defects, Twain has contributed one enduring masterpiece to our literary heritage. It alone is no mean achievement.

In the end, after threshing out the chaff of Twain's inferior work, a considerable residue remains. The worth of this remaining work can best be symbolized in terms of the dream that figures so largely in Twain's thinking. In this work he has something worthwhile to tell us about the elemental ideals and dreams that motivate the best of mankind. His dream, as wish-fulfillment, embraces a noble vision of man as a morally responsible human being who conducts himself in the light of reason and common sense. He does not deny his folk heritage, but neither does he accept it uncritically, for it would increasingly bind him with the fetters of superstition. Man is meant to be free, and he attains his freedom by voluntarily circumscribing it for himself. It is a not unworthy dream, and Twain's fear that it might be compromised is understandable. That he vitiated his genius in the conscious effort to subvert the dream is regrettable; that he did not succeed is testimony to the lasting power of his dream.

Twain had only one basic story to tell, the story of the folk hero. Its origin in an oral tradition is clear. His basic version of the tale finds its hero among the folk; the hero dreams of performing some action embodying one of the aspirations of the folk; the dream finally comes true, and he actually does become a hero. The basic plot embodies all the folk conceptions of what on a philosophical level may be referred to as the problem of appearance and reality. The dream is an elemental phenomenon fraught with awful significance for the primitive mind. As a psychic phenomenon the dream was understood by the folk mind, centuries before Freud, as wish-fulfillment. It has been projected upon mankind's culture to represent the ideas and aspirations the group wished for its future, and thus the dream also has the force of prophecy as well. Dreams change, of course, with the dreamer, but at any given moment in society there is always a disparity between the cultural dream, with its attendant myths, and actuality. Why such a disparity should exist has troubled the minds of men both on the level of the folk and that of their intellectual leaders since the beginning of history. It is the problem to which Twain addressed himself, consciously in formulating over a period of many years his deterministic body of ideas and, perhaps more significantly for his art, unconsciously in projecting the problem in artistic terms of primitive character reckoning with moral problems on his own level in his own culture.

In Twain's first novel, *The Gilded Age*, the dream story is told in fragmentary form through the several subplots, but its main lines can be traced. The dream of sudden wealth, the pot of gold at the end of the rainbow, is an unworthy dream. Immorally won wealth is gilt; true gold is the product of honest effort. Thus is affirmed the morality of the folk embodied in folk wisdom. Following it and unhampered by the terms of collaboration, *Tom Sawyer* is a better expression of the story. Twain allowed himself to flex his realistic style upon a range of material more appropriate to his story. As a "hymn to boyhood," *Tom Sawyer* pictures Tom as the eternal symbol of the primitive mind as it occurs in boys close to the folk rather than those reared in a nursery. Tom's dreams are elemental even for the folk mind—to discover buried treasure, to perform a self-sacrificial act for love of his beloved, to save a life, to triumph over his enemy. All of them come true, and Tom enjoys the hero's reward—the sweet delight of admiration from his fellow man.

Huck Finn is even more of the folk than Tom, but not himself entirely uncorrupted by books. Jim, however, is not so contaminated, and from him Huck respectfully learns. He defers to Jim's superior experience and ultimately learns moral responsibility by casting off false pride. Huck's adventure is greater than Tom's because Huck's dream is a nobler one. It is not a conscious dream, but Huck nonetheless searches for an ideal society founded upon the freedom that grows out of moral responsibility. His dream is defined in terms of the societies that he rejects and from which he flees. The realities of the hypocrisy of the Widow Douglas' household, of Pap Finn's primitive bestiality, of the irrational convention of feuding—all these Huck rejects; and not until the raffish Duke and King come aboard does the reader perhaps realize that Huck's dream had come true on the raft in the family society of Jim, the father, and Huck, the son, and the spirit of the river floating free. It is no wonder that Tom's petty and hypocritical dream at the conclusion comes as an anticlimax. It does, however, reinforce by contrast the nobility of the dream that was dreamed on the journey down the river.

The Prince and the Pauper, *A Connecticut Yankee*, and *An American Claimant* take up the basic folk tale, but more directly project the dream upon society. Tom Canty dreams of being a prince, and his dream really does come true; but in it he also is thrust into the position of recognizing the injustice done to the common man, the folk from which he sprang. He envisages a more enlightened legal system based upon mercy, and the reader is kept aware of the disparity between then and now and of the fact that the dream of equality before the law has come true in our own day. But Twain was evidently troubled by the contrast he presented, for he took up a continuation of the dream in *A Connecticut Yankee*. This dream is of heroic proportions—to create an ideal society—a dream that was to be realized in the nineteenth century. His dream came true, but unfortunately the contrast kept backfiring. The nineteenth century was more profoundly tarnished than Twain realized in *The Gilded Age*, and *An American Claimant*, though it is a muddled performance as a novel, is an ironic admission of the betrayal of the dream upon which America was founded.

During these years, when he was writing *A Connecticut Yankee* and for some time thereafter, Twain was formulating his pessimistic philosophy; at the same time, the society he moved in was separating Twain from his folk heritage. His conscious philosophy inevitably was brought to bear upon the forces with which he was reckoning in his art. With *Pudd'nhead Wilson* and *Tom Sawyer Abroad*, he turned once again to the earlier versions of his story. He picked up Tom enjoying the last remnants of reward as a hero and set him off on another adventure in an airship that would again make him a hero. But now the folk tale is no longer organic; it is nothing more than a device, a frame within which Twain explores the primitive folk mind, revealing its richness and complexity, but not fully appreciating its wisdom and common sense.

Pudd'nhead Wilson by contrast is written to a thesis dictated by his philosophy. The villagers serve as a mob chorus demonstrating the worst Pap Finn aspects of the folk mind; Wilson is the spokesman for Twain's rational views, but his dream of restoring his reputation is on the scale of Tom Sawyer's. It is entirely selfish and motivated not by sympathy or compassion, but by derision of his fellow man; his triumph is a minor one. Roxy is left, and her dream is unfulfilled, her freedom won only through tragic suffering.

Twain's maturity was long delayed, and the disillusion consequently all the more bitter when he came to realize that one's dreams do not always come true, perhaps can never come true. In the frustration of his disillusion, he tried passionately in *Joan of Arc* to insist upon dedication and fidelity to the moral vision within each individual. Finally, in *The Mysterious Stranger*, he surrendered completely to his disillusion by asserting that perhaps the dream is all we have; it is the only reality.

In telling his story the only discipline Twain had for controlling his material was his realistic style, which made him render the general forces he was trying to control into concrete, specific, accurate prose. It was a limited realistic style, however, not deliberately conceived by Twain as anything more than the clothing of his thought, the manner of his expression having little to do with matter. It might have continued to serve Twain well had he confined himself to his true range of material, but the fact remains that he did not. The telling of his folk tale led him to subject it to the scrutiny of his later philosophy, itself the product of only half-assimilated intellectual concepts. The tale did not ring true to him under such a critical examination; he was forced to rewrite it, and he did not have the necessary equipment. His style of realism was a projection of an early shrewd, natively intelligent, primitive mind incapable of dealing significantly with a sophisticated problem; it was also the fixed projection of a limited range of material. To demand that he change in his declining years was asking too much of Twain. The damage was done by the attempt to change.

Twain's artistic ordeal, decline, and fall are the product of his partial desertion of the folk mind without a gain in adequate sophisticated self-control. The true range of Mark Twain's genius was in exploring the American mind in circumstances he knew best. He did not fully realize that when he stepped outside of this area of experience, his style would have to be modified to fit altered conditions.

Perhaps one example among many possible ones will illustrate. Twain's favorite device for gaining comic effect was to have his narrator entirely unaware of the absurdity of his story. He expounds the point in "How to Tell a Story," and his "Jumping Frog" is an early instance of an effective use of the device. Part of Huck's charm often lies in this same unawareness. In his early successes Twain found it a sure way to exploit the basic humor of a situation without realizing why it was an effective device. Therefore, at one point in *Joan of Arc* when he wished to inject a little comic relief, he called upon this time-tested strategy. He has Joan's scribe report her uncle's tale of riding a bull to a funeral. Thus Twain has the opportunity of capitalizing upon the naïveté of both narrators. The incident does not succeed, however, for its very use is absurd in this instance. Inadvertently Twain's simple French peasants become a pair of transplanted Obedstown innocents abroad in a big city. The reader's sense of what is fitting under the circumstances is offended.

Not so grossly perhaps, but in numerous other instances the rhetoric and style of *Huckleberry Finn* are misapplied in later stories in different settings. We must conclude that Twain simply did not realize how closely his style was wedded to the environment and intellect of the folk he knew best; and being unaware, he could not understand the modifications necessary for effecting a successful break with the folk mind in applying his later mechanistic doctrines.

II

Humor and Realism

A GOOD DEFINITION of humor is hard to find. The literature on the subject is as unsatisfactory as it is bulky, marked chiefly by an absence of the subject under discussion. But it is enough for our purpose simply to say that whenever Twain affects the risibilities of his readers he is humorous. This view makes allowance for the ephemeral character of much of his humor. Aging corpses and seasickness may be very funny subjects for some types of mind; indeed, these examples are evidence of Twain's appeal to the uncultivated mind that would not otherwise read anything at all; or they may simply be lapses of taste on Twain's part. At any rate, if we grant that humor is fundamental to Twain's style, this definition allows us to account for his failures as well as his successes in terms of the permanence and value of his humor. Stephen Leacock has tried to define this sort of humor:

> The humor that we call American is based on seeing things as they are, as apart from history, convention, and prestige, and thus introducing sudden and startling contrasts as between things as they are supposed to be—revered institutions, accepted traditions, established conventions—and things as they are. Like many other things this humor came out of the west, beyond the plains. You had to get clear away from civilization to start it. . . . This ability to see things as they are became the basis of new American humor. It is embodied in Mark Twain's *Innocents Abroad* more than in any other book. But it lies at the basis of the work of all the "school," if one can give such a name to people who hardly went there. When Mark Twain's *Connecticut Yankee* speaks of the armor of a knight as "hardware," he is seeing it as no one could see it who was used to calling it bassinet, gorget, greaves, and hawberk.[1]

The humor described by Leacock we have come to associate with Twain at his best; but Twain also was a satirist. Satire, of course, is often achieved in this sort of humor, and in Huck's humorous irony and understatement, the effect of satire is achieved without the bark and sting so often associated with satire. Twain's later satire is not so subtly achieved and more often seeks its effect without the tempering smile of humor, and when accompanied by humor, the satire tends to overwhelm the comic and render it painful rather than pleasant. *An American Claimant*, for example, is seriously marred in this respect. One is forced to judge Twain in these later instances on the basis of the ideas informing his satire and to find his effects unacceptable on the grounds of the error of his assumptions and his fundamental misconception of the nature of humor.

This last point requires some comment, since general opinion has held that of all aspects of his craft, humor was the one Twain most consciously controlled. It is true that Twain was conscious to a high degree of the tricks and devices of a certain type of humor, but he gave little thought to humor as anything more than the sugar coating of a bitter pill of truth. He seems generally to have regarded humor as the handmaid of satire rather than as a legitimate end in itself. But often, despite Twain's apparent conscious view, humor does become an end in itself in his best work.

A consideration of matters relating to the values within his humor is relevant in this connection. If we assume that lasting humor is more valuable than transitory humor, it is appropriate to ask what elements of his humor still are treasured, what parts of it still promise some degree of permanence. Twain himself offered an explanation:

> Humorists of the "mere" sort cannot survive. Humor is only a fragrance, a decoration. Often it is merely an odd trick of speech and of spelling. . . . Humor must not professedly teach, and it must not professedly preach, but it must do both if it would live forever. By forever I mean thirty years. With all its preaching it is not likely to outlive so long a term as that. The very things it preaches about, and which are novelties when it preaches about them, can cease to be novelties and become commonplaces in thirty years.[2]

Besides demonstrating a degree of consciousness toward his writing, this passage also shows considerable insight into the satiric function of humor. Unlike the host of mere humorists he discusses, he assigns the value and permanence of humor to the subject it adorns. The error of his reasoning in this passage is that he regards the subject of humor as something of topical interest rather than as some permanent foible or trait of human behavior. The error is reflected in his practice. He burlesqued a now-forgotten person or book oftener than he satirized a more permanent trait or attitude. It is the latter we now treasure, in spite of the former. This was the danger of humor for Twain, that an unimportant subject could be made just as entertaining and funny as a more valuable subject.

Unfortunately, Twain's success as a humorist contributed to hamper his discovery of his more lasting and important range of subject matter. Only very late in his life did he appreciate the value of *Huckleberry Finn,* for example, and even then he really preferred *Joan of Arc.* We can deprecate this lack of perception, but considering Twain's audience and his role as a humorist, one can perhaps excuse him for not knowing his best subject in 1874, when he began to apply his talent to the writing of novels. His audience had found his description of Brigham Young at home with a stupendous family just as funny as Scotty Briggs arranging for Buck Fanshaw's funeral, and certainly in his day a much more interesting subject. Mormon polygamy is a forgotten issue today, but Scotty Briggs is still a humorous character and promises to remain so for a long time.

To accuse Twain of not knowing the difference between the two examples, however, would not be entirely correct. He often indicated that he thought humor and satire to be one and the same, as in the observation he made regarding humorists of the mere sort; and he was, of course, in error—humor and satire may exist independent of one another. Indeed, the greatest examples of satire seem to have made only a limited use of humor. When he wrote "How to Tell a Story" (1893), he realized the difference between comedy and humor, for he points out that the story he uses as an example is raised from the level of comedy to humor by the author's creation of a humorous character as narrator. The realization came too late, for most of Twain's novels show an apparent lack of discrimination between comedy, burlesque, satire, and humor. We still laugh, though perhaps not as heartily as his contemporaries, at much of the mixture, but it is his humor that we most value.

Although in "How to Tell a Story" Twain seemed aware of a difference between comedy and humor, he was not fully conscious of what that difference was. He is correct in finding humor richer and more satisfying than wit and jokes, but he is incomplete in his attempt at defining why this is so. His example of James Whitcomb Riley's "dull-witted old farmer" illustrates the difference well, but Twain errs in thinking the source of humor lies chiefly in the devices of its narration.

> To string incongruities and absurdities together in a wandering and sometimes purposeless way, and seem innocently unaware that they are absurdities, is the basis of the American art, if my position is correct. Another feature is the slurring of the point. A third is dropping of a studied remark apparently without knowing it, as if one were thinking aloud. The fourth is the pause.[3]

These things may often be true of humor, particularly the oral variety, but they are only symptomatic. What actually has taken place is the creation of a character based upon incongruity that does not clash significantly with reality placed in circumstances also involving some basic incongruity or paradox. The humor lies in contemplating a type of character in a somewhat ridiculous situation rather than merely in the tricks by which the story is narrated.

The important thing to observe is that such humor gains its effect by keeping always in close touch with reality. The difficulties of Brigham Young hilariously plagued by problems incited by a plethora of wives and children is funny because it multiplies and exaggerates the same very real problems of more common monogamous marriages. The reader supplies the incongruity of the situation; without the norm of reality to provide contrast, the incident would not be funny. But the Scotty Briggs situation is more satisfying because the incongruous misunderstanding does not at all depart from reality; it is much more believable. In addition, the character of Scotty is very real. He is eccentric, of course; that is why he is humorous. But he is not a freak. He is a character whose exaggerated behavior sets him humorously apart from his fellows, but his original might well have actually existed.

The humor of character and situation approaches greatness when another element is added, what Stephen Leacock calls an atmosphere of pathos. It is present to a marked degree, for example, in Dickens' best work. The humor of character and situation tempers the underlying pity for human suffering. As Leacock says, it is "humor in which the pathos of life in general is the basis—the incongruous contrast between the eager fret of our life and its final nothingness." [4] We should add that such humor requires great skill and, above all, restraint in its execution. If the right tone is not struck, pathos becomes bathos, as happens so often in Dickens, but rarely with Twain. His aversion to sentimentalism led him rather to tip the scale in the opposite direction; humor was more likely to break from a gentle smile into burlesque at the expense of pathos.

In his early work Twain did show some indication of later achievement in this direction of skillfully blending humor and pathos. "A True Story," though probably written as late as 1874, will serve to illustrate. The plot is simple; it is an old Negro woman's droll and matter-of-fact story of how she and her children had been separated by sale at auction and of how years later she was finally reunited with her youngest son. Her narrative had been prompted by Twain's comment upon her carefree good humor and the apparent lack of trouble in her life. In other hands the account might easily have emerged as a sentimental commentary on an old Negro's misfortune or perhaps a passionate indictment of slavery. Save for the ironic statement made by the woman at the end, however, comment is reserved. "Oh, no Misto C_____, I hain't had no trouble. An' no joy!" In this respect it anticipates many of the episodes in *Huckleberry Finn*. The story is the highest form of the humor of character and situation with an underlying theme of pathos. It is, therefore, astonishing to find Twain referring to the sketch in a letter to Howells in the following terms:

I enclose also "A True Story," which has no humor in it. You can pay as lightly as you choose for that, if you want it, for it is rather out of my line. I have not altered the old colored woman's story except to begin at the beginning, instead of the middle, as she did—and traveled both ways.[5]

Twain obviously is serious in this statement, since he is willing to suffer in his pocket. The story is not typical of his early work, because with admirable restraint he resists any temptation to moralize; the story speaks for itself and is a more subtle display of technique than he had shown before. The same restraint and careful selection of detail was later to mark *Huckleberry Finn*. Twain's remarks indicate that the story is founded upon fact in accord with his desire for realism, but at the same time he reveals a remarkable ignorance regarding the humor of the piece. Not to recognize the humor of this story speaks eloquently of Twain's fundamental lack of understanding of the very basis of his art. Just as when he said that "Humor is only a fragrance, a decoration," here he demonstrates that, although he desired to employ humor in his work, he was limited in his understanding of it.

In the discussion of Twain's humor, its closeness to actuality has been a secondary theme. And in the best examples, actuality was a part of Twain's experience gained not by conscious observation but by the unconscious absorption of his early years. Remaining close to his own experience was a deliberate part of Twain's craft, and this view of experience was central to his conscious beliefs about literary creative activity.

Twain tells us how experience molded his style and became part of his method. When asked to contribute to a volume published in 1890, this is what he wrote:

Your inquiry has set me thinking, but, so far, my thought fails to materialize. I mean that, upon consideration, I am not sure that I have methods in composition. I do suppose I have—I suppose I must have—but they somehow refuse to take shape in my mind; their details refuse to separate and submit to classification and description; they remain a jumble—visible, like the fragments of glass when you look in at the wrong end of a kaleidoscope, but still a jumble. If I could turn the whole thing around and look in at the other end, why then the figures would flash into form out of the chaos, and I shouldn't have any more trouble. But my head isn't right for that today, apparently. It might have been, maybe, if I had slept last night.

However, let us try guessing. Let us guess that whenever we read a sentence and like it, we unconsciously store it away in our model-chamber; and it goes with a myriad of its fellows to the building, brick by brick, of the eventual edifice which we call our style. And let us guess that whenever we run across other forms—bricks—whose color, or some other defect, offends us, we unconsciously reject these, and so one never finds them in our edifice.

If I have subjected myself to any training processes, and no doubt I have, it must have been in this unconscious or half-conscious fashion. I think it unlikely that deliberate and consciously methodical training is usual with the craft. I think it likely that the training most in use is of this unconscious sort, and is guided and governed and made by-and-by unconsciously systematic, by an automatically-working taste, a taste which selects and rejects without asking you for any help, and patiently and steadily improves itself without troubling you to approve or applaud. Yes, and likely enough when the structure is at last pretty well up, and attracts attention, YOU feel complimented, whereas you didn't build it, and didn't even consciously superintend.

Yes; one notices, for instance, that long, involved sentences confuse him, and that he is obliged to re-read them to get the sense. Unconsciously, then, he rejects that brick. Unconsciously he accustoms himself to writing short sentences as a rule. At times he may indulge himself with a long one, but he will make sure that there are no folds in it, no vaguenesses, no parenthetical interruptions of its view as a whole; when he is done with it, it won't be a sea-serpent, with half its arches under the water, it will be a torchlight procession.

Well, also he will notice in the course of time, as his reading goes on, that the difference between the almost right word and the right word is really a large matter—'tis the difference between the lightening-bug and the lightening. After that, of course, that exceedingly important brick, the exact word—however, this is running into an essay, and I beg pardon. So I seem to have arrived at this: doubtless I have methods, but they begot themselves, in which case I am only their proprietor, not their father.[6]

Experience not only forms his style, but also provides the subject matter for the writer. In his essay "What Paul Bourget Thinks of Us," he lauds the role of the novelist in society and reflects the importance of the competent novelist's experience, for it is the very substance of his art.

Does the native American novelist try to generalize the nation? No, he lays plainly before you the ways and speech and life of a few people grouped in a certain place—his own place—and that is one book. In time he and his brethren will report to you the life and the people of the whole nation—the life of a group in a New England village; . . . then the farm-life in fifty States and Territories; a hundred patches of life and groups of people in a dozen widely separated cities. And the Indians will be attended to; . . . and the negroes; and the Idiots and Congressmen; . . . the Irish, . . . the Baptists, . . . the Moonshiners. And when a thousand able novels have been written, *there* you have the soul of the people; and not anywhere else can these be had. And the shadings of characters, manners, feelings, ambitions, will be infinite.

This testament to the importance of the role which the novelist plays does not accord with any notion of Twain deprecating his profession or his activity as a novelist. It does suggest that Twain differed from other novelists in the experience and segment of life that he recorded. But to say that he was aware of his difference from other writers is not to say that he believed himself to be inferior. The evidence shows no more than that he was modest concerning his professional attainments. So far as is possible to determine such an attitude, Twain actually seems to have been proud of the recognition given him as a professional man of letters. He chafed at what he felt to be a too confining reputation as a "mere humorist," and, though he was modest concerning his own achievement, he honored the profession in which he held a minor position. Later in the same essay Twain more explicitly relates the novelist's own first-hand experience to his accomplishment by assigning it the key position in the competent novelist's method.

The Observer of Peoples has to be a Classifier, a Grouper, a Deducer, a Generalizer, a Psychologizer; and, first and last, a Thinker. He has to be all these, and when he is at home, observing his own folk, he is often able to prove competency. But history has shown that when he is abroad observing unfamiliar people the chances are heavily against him. He is then a naturalist observing a bug, with no more than a naturalist's chance of being able to tell the bug anything new about himself, and no more than a naturalist's chance of being able to teach it any new ways which it will prefer to its own.

A foreigner can photograph the exteriors of a nation, but I think that that is as far as he can get. I think that no foreigner can report its interior—its soul, its life, its speech, its thought. I think that a knowledge of these is acquirable in only one way; not two or four or six—absorption; years and years of unconscious absorption; years and years of intercourse with the life concerned. . . . Observation? Of what real value is it? One learns peoples through the heart, not the eyes or the intellect.

There is only one expert who is qualified to examine the souls and the life of a people and make a valuable report—the native novelist. . . . This native specialist is not qualified to begin work until he has been absorbing during twenty-five years. How much of his competency is derived from conscious "observation"? The amount is so slight that it counts for next to nothing in the equipment. Almost the whole capital of the novelist is the slow accumulation of *un*conscious observation—absorption.

One may see that in this passage Twain anticipates the weakness of the pseudo-scientific method of the naturalists in fiction. Scientific objectivity may have a certain usefulness, but it is limited to externals and cannot make any valuable contribution to an understanding of our interiors. Obviously, to be successful, such a method must be supplemented by the writer's personal insight into character, and this is not achieved except through long experience. But of more importance, the quotation illuminates the point that, though his style seems devoted to the selection of concrete surface detail, Twain's ultimate concern is with the interior reality. His way of getting at this truth is the careful selection of surface details (appearance) that all together point unmistakably to the underlying truth (reality).

Experience was also one of the most important elements in the criteria by which Twain judged the work of others. In writing to William Dean Howells about an installment of one of his novels appearing in a magazine, Twain offered this enthusiastic comment:

That's the best drunk scene—because the truest—that I ever read. There are touches in it that I never saw any writer take note of before. And they are set before the reader with amazing accuracy. How very drunk, and how recently drunk, and how altogether admirably drunk you must have been to enable you to contrive that masterpiece! [7]

To a would-be writer in 1885, he wrote:

> Literature is an *art*, not an inspiration. . . . And its capital is experience—and you are too young, yet, to have much of that in your bank to draw from. . . . Is it hypercritical to notice these little blemishes? No—not in this case: for I wish to impress upon you this truth: that the moment you venture outside your *own* experience, you are in peril—don't do it.[8]

The last comment assumes ironic overtones when one calls to mind the many subsequent occasions on which Twain departed from this principle. He could not always follow the advice he so sagely dispensed to others.

Equally incongruous was a later similar dictum that he laid down concerning the necessity for founding upon a fact in one's personal experience. At that time he was engaged in writing one of his most fantastic novels, *A Connecticut Yankee*, but apparently he saw no contradiction between his practice and the observation he recorded in his notebook:

> If you attempt to create a wholly imaginary incident, adventure, or situation, you will go astray and the artificiality of the thing will be detectable, but if you found on a *fact* in your personal experience it is an acorn, a root, and every created adornment that grows out of it, and spreads its foliage and blossoms to the sun will seem reality, not invention.[9]

Such a method founds upon fact, but eschews slavish adherence to the literal fact. "I don't know anything that mars good literature so completely as too much truth. Facts contain a deal of poetry, but you can't use too many of them without damaging your literature." [10] This observation certainly argues for a considerable amount of awareness on his part, for one of the elementary lessons the would-be storyteller must learn is that an event that actually happened may be unbelievable in fiction. "Truth is stranger than fiction, but it is because Fiction is obliged to stick to possibilities; Truth isn't." [11] Of course, not all fiction must stick to possibilities, but it is a fundamental principle of realistic fiction that incidents and adornments must seem reality.

This concern for a factual basis for events in fiction was not confined to Twain's initial conception of his story and incidents, but was extended to his characters as well. His letters and autobiographical statements abound with admissions that most of his characters existed in life.[12] That he was heavily indebted to childhood associations and members of his family for the originals of characters is commonplace knowledge. But his full indebtedness has not yet been thoroughly explored. A deliberate dependence upon life for his characters was a part of his theory of fiction and he was quick to criticize "pure creation" of characters. Twain himself was not above criticism in this respect. On the occasions when he ignored his own advice, modified and even abandoned his characteristic style, he met with only indifferent success. It would almost appear that Twain was attempting to transcend the limitations of his style in order to transmute his personal experience into a more universal and meaningful statement of the truth his experience held. The attempt more often failed than not, but, it must be insisted, not alone because he partially abandoned his realism.

Realism is by no means the only successful style by which literary truth may be conveyed. Twain's later decline in significant application of a realistic style must be sought in other matters than the simple fact of abandoning a technique. It is associated rather with a consequent inability to replace the assumptions of his early style of realism with adequate substitutes in his developing philosophy. Twain's view of the importance of experience to his art did not change; what did change was his evaluation of his experience. At any rate, the important fact about Twain's view of experience is that the writer does not acquire it by objectively and passively observing life, but by actively participating in it. To a great extent it accounts for the dynamic quality of Twain's statement in fiction.

III

The Gilded Age:
A Mirror of Experience

OF ALL Twain's novels *The Gilded Age* shows the closest dependence upon his own experience. But this pronouncement is not to be construed as saying that his art attempted to be merely a mirror held up to life. Despite Twain's footnote to the contrary, the social call payed to Laura by Mrs. Patrique Oreille and other members of Washington society is a parody of actuality rather than an attempt to reproduce an actual situation. But in the gathering up of details and focusing upon a fact of that society, Twain clearly intended that the situation should reflect the essential truth of the experience. In an ironic footnote Twain reassures the reader that "it [the conversation] is scarcely in any respect an exaggeration of one which one of us listened to in an American drawing-room."

The events he records from his experience are not as they occur in actual life. They are rendered as he wishes to present them, as he sees their essential nature in the life he experienced, not as they merely seem to be on the surface. The inner reality rather than surface appearance is always his paramount concern. The chief instrument for accomplishing this aim is his style, an apparent contradiction because his style seems to deal primarily with the surface texture of life rather than its real substance. But closer examination of Twain's style reveals that it is a technique of selecting concrete, relevant details which separately form the appearance of reality—the details accurately reflect actuality; but

33

the composition, the sum of the details, focuses upon the true state of affairs underlying the surface.

In the final analysis, the great value he placed upon his personal experience lies at the core of Twain's thinking and its projection in his style. As is characteristic of most unsophisticated minds, Twain was disposed to rely heavily upon his own experience. Even when it ran counter to authority or scientific evidence, he still was inclined to retain his belief in his own contrary experience. His biographer, Paine, recounts how on one occasion he characteristically opposed a friend's rational demonstration that no matter how he turned into his curving driveway, his carriage would still present the same side to the door of the house. Periodically for years after Twain would draw diagrams and puzzle over them in the vain effort to support what he felt his own experience to have been. He apparently sincerely regarded himself as being a microcosm encompassing within his own character and experience something of the character of all men and all experience.

In a great measure *The Gilded Age* succeeds in translating to the longer form of the novel the vitality and vigor manifested in the earlier sketches and travel books. The faults of the book are largely the result of failure to integrate the ingredients in a controlling design demanded by the form of the novel. This failure cannot be blamed entirely upon his collaboration with Charles Dudley Warner. It resulted as much from Twain's own violation of, or perhaps lack of skill in conforming to, his principles of composition. Thus *The Gilded Age* stands as a spotty and fragmentary achievement. When it is bad, and much of it is, the best that can be said is that it *is* funny. Unlike most generally bad books, however, this one is rewarding reading for its picture of an age whose name has been furnished by the title. And in *The Gilded Age* Twain created his first full-length humorous character.

Of course, the book was handicapped from the start by the collaboration of two writers who not only were inexperienced in working together but who were also unpracticed in the art of the novel. Upon the evidence of the book alone one might say the authors were really unsure of their intention. Actually they believed they were quite sure of what they were about, but the fact does not alter the result. The book reads as if the authors had not made up their minds as to what sort of book they were writing; because they were aiming to do so many things, their shots scattered.

Considering the many intentions motivating the book, one marvels that it holds together at all. First, the authors were going to prove a point to their wives. Indeed, their wives played no small part in the actual writing, often serving as a sort of editorial board to choose between alternate versions written by Twain and Warner.[1] Knowing Twain, we may also assume that they were influenced by the possible financial returns. And, since the occasion for beginning the novel had been the authors' criticism of certain works of popular romantic fiction, they inevitably considered the best improvement on that sort of fiction to be a parody of its plots and themes.

As long as they were embarked upon a course of satire, they might as well range wider and attack the sentimentality and romanticism associated with most popular fiction of the day. But the intention apparently had no limit; while about it they might as well burlesque and satirize the social manifestations of these views, and there were many other social questions, such as women's rights and political corruption, they might expose. The latter course suggested that the subject might be treated realistically to the extent that they would honestly attempt to picture the age by using events closely founded upon facts. With so many rows to hoe, it is not surprising that Twain and his partner often became confused and gave the impression of a pair of amateurs at work.

Twain's early chapters, on the whole, are the best, although there are occasional parts in the rest of the book that show merit. But even these early chapters (I-XI) begin to show signs by chapter X of an inconsistency in narrative point of view. When Twain, after Warner's interruption, begins again in chapter XXIV, he is off writing a travel book about Washington, and only a few paragraphs toward the end advance the narrative. And indeed there is a great deal of plot to advance—too much—and it was as much by accident as by design that minor plots were suspended for many chapters and some even left incomplete and forgotten. The appendix apologizing for not finding Laura's father was an afterthought turning a dangling plot into a satiric statement on such plots in romantic novels.

The two writers were clowning throughout the book and did not worry about such improbabilities. The necessity for distorting and changing characters (notably that of Laura) to fit the exigencies of the plot, for example, gave the authors no serious concern. Indeed, the fault itself was turned to account as a satiric observation of just such character manipulation in the novels they intended to parody. Too often parts and even whole chapters contributed nothing to the central plot or theme. Chapter V of volume II, for example, is entirely devoted to satirizing the ignorance of bookstore clerks, for which purpose Laura is made to appear somewhat more erudite and bookish than either before or after the episode.

Fewer faults than these have condemned many books. The fact that *The Gilded Age* was an unqualified popular, if not critical, success is testimony to Twain's power. The novelty and excellence of his humor and his fresh viewpoint made it a worthwhile reading experience in spite of the faults, and certainly his performance foreshadows the excellence of those later books that more skillfully exploited the veins of humor and realism.

The aspect of his manner most striking in this first novel is the great amount of Twain's personal experience. Character, setting, and events all depict actualities, and most of them are drawn from his own past. Exactly how much Twain relied upon actual fact probably cannot accurately be known, but it seems certain that he invented and manufactured little, rather adorning and reporting material already at hand in his memory. A full catalogue is impossible, but a partial list of what seems for certain to be dependence upon actual life will serve to show the extent of his indebtedness to his experience.

The first eleven chapters are largely events autobiographical in origin. In the first chapter the reader is introduced to East Tennessee, from which Twain's parents had moved to Missouri. Paine accounts for Twain's familiarity with the scene, even though he had never visited there.

In *The Gilded Age* we have Mark Twain's picture of Squire Hawkins and Obedstown, written from descriptions supplied in later years by his mother and his brother Orion; and, while not exact in detail, it is not regarded as an exaggerated presentation of East Tennessee conditions at that time.[2]

Twain himself said, "I have written about Jamestown in *The Gilded Age* a book of mine, but it was from hearsay, not from personal knowledge."[3]

The Hawkins family was Twain's own except for Laura, and she, at least in name, was drawn from an early sweetheart who Paine says was also the original of Becky Thatcher.[4] Many of the events the family had experienced in real life are also reflected; the Tennessee land, which provides a major theme of the book, is such an example. In his autobiography Twain spoke of it in real life:

My father left a fine estate behind him in the region of Jamestown—75,000 acres. When he died in 1847 he had owned it about twenty years.... He had always said that the land would not become valuable in his time; but that it would be a commodious provision for his children some day. ... I shall have occasion to mention this land again now and then, as I go along, for it influenced our life in one way or another during more than a generation. Whenever things grew dark it rose and put out its hopeful Sellers hand and cheered us up, and said, "Do not be afraid—trust in me—wait." It kept us hoping and hoping during forty years, and forsook us at last. It put our energies to sleep and made visionaries of us—dreamers and indolent. We were always going to be rich next year—no occasion to work. It is good to begin life poor; it is good to begin life rich—these are wholesome; but to begin it poor and *prospectively* rich! The man who has not experienced it cannot imagine the curse of it.[5]

Chapter IV concerning the steamboat race and wreck contains some of Twain's most vivid writing and is obviously based upon his personal experience. A good idea of his reliance upon fact may be gained by comparing his description of the wreck toward the end of this chapter with the account of his brother's death under similar circumstances in *Life on the Mississippi*. Similarly, his description of Colonel Sellers is really a transcription from real life; his mother's cousin James Lampton was the original.

Many persons regarded Colonel Sellers as a fiction, and invention, an extravagant impossibility, and did me the honor to call
him a "creation"; but they were mistaken. I merely put him on
paper as he was; he was not a person who could be exaggerated.
The incidents which looked most extravagant, both in the book
and on the stage, were not inventions of mine, but were facts of
his life; and I was present when they were developed. John T.
Raymond's audiences used to come near to dying with laughter
over the turnip-eating scene; but, extravagant as the scene was,
it was faithful to the facts, in all its absurd details. The thing happened in Lampton's own house, and I was present.[6]

The Washington, D.C., scenes reflect the same experience he
wrote about partially in *Roughing It*. The incidents and many of
the characters were taken from fact. Senator Dilworthy, for example, was based upon Senator Pomeroy of Kansas. These later
chapters, however, generally do not continue the promise of the
early ones. The interest derives not from a continuation of his
early statement, but from a contrasting method and purpose of
expression. Where the humor of the first part depended upon
character and situation, the latter portions depend upon scattered
satiric barbs and burlesque.

Twain's initial contribution to the joint effort was an effective
mixture of realism and humor, but his later chapters are based
upon more recent experience and thus are less objectively assimilated because they lack the perspective of distance in time.
The earlier writing is better; it does not show the pressure of
circumstances forcing it to be written. Paine indicates that much
of this early portion had been written before the book was projected, whereas later chapters were often hastily written for a
deadline to be submitted to his partner. The suggestion appears to
be correct, since the early portions do not adhere closely to the
satiric intentions of the later sections.

Though, as was suggested, distance lends perspective, and the
early material was from Twain's more distant experience, the
difference in excellence does not lie in this fact alone. The humor
of the early and late chapters is significantly different in kind.
Written largely without other purpose than to tell a story enter-
tainingly, the first chapters humorously contemplate the narrated
events. The humor had its source in pathos rather than indigna-

tion. Much later and characteristically after the fact, Twain apparently understood something of the nature of this sort of humor, for in 1897 he wrote: "Everything human is pathetic. The secret source of humor itself is not joy but sorrow. There is no humor in heaven." [7] And this was after his novel-writing days. The humor of these early chapters shows a kindly tolerance of human failings, and its execution requires objectivity in presentation and restraint in comment lest it become maudlin or ridiculous. The requisite tone is generally sustained; it rarely slips into sentimentality, such as on the occasion of the death of the French midshipman, nor is it often ridiculous, as at the death of Laura.

The most striking manifestation of this kind of humor is in the characterization of a few frontier types and, of course, Colonel Sellers. Through a few Obedstown characters perched on a fence rail discussing small matters, we get an unforgettably vivid impression of the village morality from which Squire Hawkins retreats. And in Colonel Sellers, Twain achieved his first full-length humorous character. His kinship with Simon Wheeler and other humorous creations of Twain's earlier writing is readily apparent. Sellers is not consciously quaint; he is sublimely unaware that he might be considered eccentric. The basic incongruity of character that makes him humorous is the disparity between his squalid circumstances and the fantastic world of schemes his tongue creates. The incongruity is so fundamentally human that it must be exaggerated to become humorous.

Sellers is a type, a symbol if one insists. He represents the fatal optimism of a period, the dreamer who ignores the tawdry at his feet with his gaze riveted on the will-o'-the-wisp that plays him false. He is so taken up with possibilities that he cannot see actualities. His foil is Washington Hawkins, who is ultimately brought to see things as they are, while Sellers persists in pursuing his dreams to the very end. Sellers remains consistent, and he remains a humorous character because his creator does not condescend to manipulate him or tell the reader what judgments to make about him. Twain is the disinterested observer as far as Sellers is concerned.

Those critics who would have us believe that Twain was preeminently the moralizer are wrong. On the contrary, it is precisely when Twain refrains from moralizing that his effects are most convincing and successful. This is not to deny that Twain was a moralist. Certainly he expects his reader to discern the moral issue involved in Sellers' character, but the lesson is so plain that it is not necessary for Twain to dwell at length on the obvious inference. He lets the character speak for itself, and his meaning is more artistically effective.

It is when Twain's passions are aroused and blended with his humor that humor gives way to burlesque, the forcedly comic, the consciously satiric. The reader wishes he had remained calmer. Successful satire, of course, is informed by passion, but it is passion kept under rigid control lest it become mere fulmination and diatribe; or, in the case of a humorist, lest it turn to cruelty and exposition of the merely ludicrous without any of the mitigating kindness that resolves the painful apprehension of reality into gentle resignation and acceptance. At its best Twain's humor was capable of achieving this disinterest. At other times it was in the service of satire, which differs from humor chiefly in the fact that it actively seeks a reformation of human frailty through criticism. Humor is only one device by which satire may achieve its purpose. This difference between humor and satire may be granted, but the line of distinction is difficult to draw, since it may be argued that the difference is one of degree. The incongruity basic to humor always requires at least an implicit norm of reality so that incongruity, or deviation from the norm, may be apparent. One may then see that satire is always latent in humor, only awaiting a slight gesture to affirm or deny the norm of reality. So long as the gesture is withheld and the writer exercises restraint, humor results, but humor gives way to satire in almost the exact measure that the author reveals his ethical purpose.

The book has often been praised as an effective satiric treatment of the corruption in Grant's administration, but it is effective only because there is scarcely any other treatment of the subject to afford comparison. Henry Adams' *Democracy*, for example, is pale and bloodless and concentrates upon a few characters without illuminating their era. Fiction may afford no comparison, but fact does, and *The Gilded Age* suffers in the light of later histories of the period. The Knobs University bill and the Columbus River Navigation project are petty cash by the side of actual swindles and the political activities of the railroad interests.

The satire is too indiscriminately scattered. The only principle of organization seems to have been to satirize almost everything as the opportunity and inclination presented themselves. The result is less than satisfactory as an analysis of the corruption of the period; and if the book pretended to be no more, we should be justified in judging it accordingly. But it also was a parody of popular novels of the period, and, viewed as such, it presents a more coherent statement than most critics have allowed. The book really makes a two-fold critical attack upon the age it portrays: it realistically and directly pictures corrupt practices, but it also indirectly shows up the age by presenting an ironic picture as it might appear in the pages of a popular romantic work. Such a reading, once the two points of view are kept in mind, reveals a consistent set of moral assumptions at the basis of the work. For Washington Hawkins discovers that the old homely virtues of industry, hard work, and honest application, dear to the heart of the folk, pay off ultimately. The idler and dreamer, no matter how grandiose his dreams, never gets ahead. And in the area of public morality, the authors' ironic preface clearly indicates that the trouble with society is in the betrayal of conventional moral standards.

> It will be seen that it [the book] deals with an entirely ideal state of society; and the chief embarrassment of the writers in this realm of the imagination has been the want of illustrative examples. In a state where there is no fever of speculation, no inflamed desire for sudden wealth, where the poor are simple-minded and contented, and the rich are all honest and generous, where society is in a condition of primitive purity, and politics is the occupation of only the capable and the patriotic, there are necessarily no materials for such a history as we have constructed out of an ideal commonwealth.

This criticism implies that man and society are capable of moral progress, that such progress lies in the direction not of achieving a new state, but rather of returning to a condition that existed at some time in the past. Thus the assumption of progress in man's affairs in *The Gilded Age* does not conflict with the essentially primitive folk notions underlying Twain's realistic portrayal of life.

IV

Tom Sawyer:
"Seeming of Reality"

TWAIN was fond of associating the imagery of painting and photography in his style. For example there is his criticism of a Bierstadt landscape. The mountains and other topographical features seemed to be as Twain remembered them in reality, but something was wrong. That something, he decided, was atmosphere; the atmosphere of the painting was not right. The style fell short of being realistic because it did not faithfully depict actuality. In this instance style concerned background or setting —the location of the subject rather than the technique of its presentation alone. Twain demanded that the setting be true, authentic, and based on the writer's experience.

Honest and accurate treatment of this aspect of style he felt was the foundation of Bret Harte's best work.

> It was in Yreka and Jackass Gulch that Harte learned to accurately observe and put with photographic exactness on paper the woodland scenery of California and the general country aspects—the stagecoach, its driver and its passengers, and the clothing and general style of the surface miner, the gambler, and their women; and it was also in these places that he learned, without the trouble of observing, all that he didn't know about mining, and how to make it read as if an expert were behind the pen. It was in those places that he also learned how to fascinate Europe and America with the quaint dialect of the miner—the dialect which no man in heaven or earth had ever used until Harte invented it.[1]

According to Twain, Harte goes astray when he violates the principles of naturalness and honesty in reporting what he has observed.

There were also other occasions on which this concern with style was associated with photography. We have already remarked that Twain seems to have admired Howells for the very qualities of realism the latter preached. Consider this example, which seems typical of Twain's genuine admiration: ". . . everywhere your pen falls it leaves a photograph." [2] On another occasion Twain had written to Howells concerning the importance of details. "I really don't see how the story of the runaway horse could read well with the little details of names and places and things left out. They are the true life of the narrative." [3] These examples stress the elements of truth, accuracy of detail, photographic quality, and fidelity to experience—even necessity for experience —that Howells also admired.

This pictorial quality that Twain admired is much in evidence in *Tom Sawyer*. In presenting each of the episodes, Twain seems to proceed almost as though he were merely reporting action as he witnessed it taking place on a stage. As a consequence, he rendered his scene in visual terms of motion and the appearance of solid objects, but there are no other sensory images present of taste or smell or touch or sound (except for dialogue). A brief analysis of the whitewashing scene will illustrate. Twain arranges only a few props—a high board fence, a brush, a bucket of whitewash, and later the articles transferred from the various victims to Tom. Thereafter the entire episode is told through verbs of action—Tom's motions as he dissembles and the behavior of his victims. If we omit the dialogue of the episode, none of which involves imagery other than that of sound, and present the remaining narrative and descriptive portions, a representative passage stands as follows:

> He took up his brush and went tranquilly to work. Ben Rogers hove in sight presently—the very boy, of all boys, whose ridicule he had been dreading. Ben's gait was the hop-skip-and-jump— proof enough that his heart was light and his anticipations high. He was eating an apple, and giving a long, melodious whoop, at intervals, followed by a deep-toned ding-dong-dong, ding-dong-dong, for he was personating a steamboat. As he drew near, he slackened speed, took the middle of the street, leaned far over to starboard and rounded to ponderously and with laborious pomp and circumstance—for he was personating the "Big Mis-

souri," and considered himself to be drawing nine feet of water. He was boat and captain and engine-bells combined, so he had to imagine himself standing on his own hurricane-deck giving the orders and executing them: . . .

The headway ran almost out and he drew up slowly toward the sidewalk. . . .

His arms straightened and stiffened down his sides. . . .

His right hand, meantime, describing stately circles,—for it was representing a forty-foot wheel. . . .

The left hand began to describe circles. . . .

Tom went on whitewashing—paid no attention to the steamboat. . . .

No answer. Tom surveyed his last touch with the eye of an artist, then he gave his brush another gentle sweep and surveyed the result, as before. Ben ranged up alongside of him. Tom's mouth watered for the apple, but he stuck to his work.

Nowhere does Twain record the feel of the heat on this summer day, the hot smell of dust, the lazy drone of insects, the wet slap and rasp of brush on boards, or the sharp, sweet taste of the apple. In the entire chapter, as here, the imagery is largely confined to visual sensations.

On the subject of more narrowly linguistic aspects of style, Twain was more explicit, but even in this more restricted view of style, grammar alone was not really as important as other qualities. Indeed, Twain was aware that he was not above reproach himself in the matter of grammar, but his use of language was a deliberate striving for colloquial ease rather than carelessness.

If I were asked an opinion I would call this an ungrammatical nation. There is no such thing as perfect grammar, and I don't always speak good grammar myself. But I have been foregathering for the past few days with professors of American universities and I've heard them all say things like this: "He don't like to do it." [4]

Twain rather feels that clarity and effectiveness of expression are most important. He praises Thomas Fuller's compactness of statement and observes, "He uses homely similes, mostly, but his meaning flashes out from them as though a drummond light had been suddenly cast upon the page." [5] And of an aspiring author's work he wrote, "It is crude, and betrays the unpracticed hand all along; . . . it wants compression—is too wordy, too diffuse." [6]

And he compliments his daughter Clara with these words: "You have style—good style—no barnacles on it in the way of unnecessary retarding words." [7] Of his own work he wrote to Howells early in his career, "In spite of myself, how awkwardly I do jumble words together; and how often I do use three words when one would answer—a thing I am always trying to guard against." [8]

The key to any good style he felt to be its vocabulary.

> A powerful agent is the right word: it lights the reader's way and makes it plain; a close approximation to it will answer, and much traveling is done in a well enough fashion by its help, but we do not welcome it and applaud it and rejoice in it as we do when *the* right one blazes out on us.[9]

Naturally a narrow vocabulary would seriously handicap the writer. Such a one he criticized by saying, "His vocabulary is too limited, and so, by consequence, descriptions suffer in the matter of variety." [10] And if he consciously called for application of the principle of variety, he still understood that the principle could be violated. Such knowledge argues for his knowing what rhetoricians taught, but fortunately he was individualist enough to escape slavish adherence to their rules.

> But in English, when we have used a word a couple of times in a paragraph, we imagine we are growing tautological and so we are weak enough to exchange it for some other word which only approximates exactness, to escape what we wrongly fancy is a greater blemish. Repetition may be bad, but surely inexactness is worse.[11]

Though Twain was fascinated by words themselves, he was well aware that they were symbols, and their significance accrued from the thing which they represented. "Words are only painted fire; a look is the fire itself." [12] Nor is the referent comprehensible without experience of its antecedent. "Things which are outside of our orbit—our own particular world—things which by our constitution and equipment we are unable to see, or feel, or otherwise experience—cannot be made comprehensible to us in words." [13] In matters of style, as with plot and character, the test always is basically one of experience.

In practice for Twain words existed largely as talk and the representation of talk. There is a studied colloquial ease about his own exposition, and the chief device of characterization he uses is conversation. "Learning began with talk and is therefore older than books." [14] One can learn a great deal about a person's mind and personality by observing the way he talks. The attempt accurately to capture the real flavor of talk as it actually existed was so much a novelty in American letters that Twain found it necessary to caution his reader in a short preface to *Huckleberry Finn*: "In this book a number of dialects are used. . . . I make this explanation for the reason that without it many readers might suppose that all these characters were trying to talk alike and not succeeding." The same care he also exercised in the rest of his prose, and much of his revision was in the direction of a more conversational tone. When a passage did not sound right in revision, he often fell back upon his natural inclination and experience as a yarn spinner and talked it out loud until the best words presented themselves. "I amend dialect stuff by talking and talking and talking it till it sounds right." [15] The logical extension of such a colloquial style was reached with the writing of his autobiography, when he abandoned the uncomfortable posture of pen in hand and settled back in bed to dictate his memories to a stenographer.

It was in the course of one of our many conversations at Onteora that Mark described to me his method of work in writing "Tom Sawyer" and "Huckleberry Finn." He declared that there was no episode in either of these stories which had not actually happened, either to himself or to one or another of the boys he had known. He began the composition of "Tom Sawyer" with certain of his boyish recollections in mind, writing on and on until he had utilized them all, whereupon he put his manuscript aside and ceased to think about it, except in so far as he might recall from time to time, and more or less unconsciously, other recollections of those early days. Sooner or later he would return to his work to make use of memories he had recaptured in the interval. After he had harvested this second crop, he again put his work away, certain that in time he would be able to call back other scenes and other situations. When at last he became convinced that he had made his profit out of every possible reminiscence, he went over what he had written with great care, adjusting the several instalments one to the other, sometimes transposing a chapter or two and sometimes writing into the earlier chapters the necessary preparation for adventures in the

later chapters unforeseen when he was engaged on the beginnings
of the book. Thus he was enabled to bestow on the completed
story a more obvious coherence than his haphazard procedure
would otherwise have attained.[16]

In Brander Matthews' account of the genesis of *Tom Sawyer*,
we can observe how the operation of Twain's unconscious cerebration recovered his material from his memory, and the same
witness further indicates the extensive revision which went into
consciously imposing some form upon the material.

Unorthodox the procedure may have been, but it hardly seems
just to call it haphazard after describing the care that Twain ex-
pended upon revision and rewriting. Haphazard suggests lucky
and accidental results, but the reverse would seem to be true.
Brander Matthews' choice of a word inconsistent with the evidence he furnishes indicates the prevalence of the myth later
made central to Van Wyck Brooks's view of Twain that he hated
revision, hastily and carelessly performing the onerous chore. It
is true that he furnishes ample testimony that he disliked correcting proof—that dull, mechanical task—but this is hardly revision.
That job was finished as part of the process of writing long before
his copy ever went to the printer. *Captain Stormfield's Visit to
Heaven*, for example, went through many revisions over the
course of nearly forty years before he was finally satisfied to
publish it. Part of his reluctance, of course, came from his fear of
being charged with "shocking and irreverent" treatment of his
subject, but his numerous alterations also indicate dissatisfaction
as well with the style of the earlier versions.

His letters also contain many references to the process of revision. Concerning *Tom Sawyer* he wrote Howells: "It is about
900 pages of MS and may be 1000 when I shall have finished
'working up' vague places." [17] And again he wrote to Howells
about "The Recent Carnival of Crimes": ". . . although it is only
70 pages MS (less than two days work, counting by bulk) I have
spent 3 more days trimming, altering and working at it. I shall
put in one more day's polishing on it." [18] Clearly revisions and
alterations were a major part of the process of writing for Twain,
and, in point of time, took as much or more labor than the original draft.

The chief drawback of this leisurely method from Twain's point of view was the fact that the required time to complete such a work was unpredictable. It might, and often did, take years to finish a novel. Such a procedure was an obvious disadvantage for a writer who depended largely upon his pen for the support of a lavish household. His travel books most strikingly show the effects of the pressure of time in the amount of padding with extensive quotations which Twain often employed merely to increase wordage and reduce the time required. But some of his novels also show evidences of deadlines to be met and were constructed according to a predetermined plan of the subject and plot. *The American Claimant*, for example, kept the plot of the original dramatic version while Twain expanded the dialogue by adding the narrative prose framework of a novel.

In *Tom Sawyer* Mark Twain went back to the material in the early chapters of *The Gilded Age*. There were the place, the time, and the people he knew best and, consequently, the material he could most meaningfully communicate. The selection of what proved to be his proper range of material was in accord with his conception of realism, for his doctrine of experience was fundamental to that conception, and the material of *Tom Sawyer* was most intimately a part of his personal experience. Moreover, Twain's treatment of his material was no less in accord with his principles of composition.

For a time Twain apparently conceived of *Tom Sawyer* as adult fare, but at Howells' suggestion he directed it primarily to boys and girls, although he still hoped that it would also appeal to a wider audience. During the period of final revisions, he wrote to Howells in July, 1875, "It is not a boy's book, at all. It will only be read by adults. It is only written for adults." [19] By November, Howells had read the book, and Twain had changed his conception of its audience. "Mrs. Clemens decides with you that the book should issue as a book for boys, pure and simple— and so do I. It is surely the correct idea." [20] His final revisions were made to conform with this different audience in mind: "I finally concluded to cut the Sunday School speech down to the first two sentences, leaving no suggestion of satire, since the book is to be for boys and girls; I tamed the various obscenities until

I judged that they no longer carried offence." [21] Actually the change of intended audience did not require much more revision; Twain indicates as much in writing to Howells. "I was careful not to inflict the MS upon you until I had thoroughly and painstakingly revised it; therefore, the only faults left were those that would discover themselves to others, not me—and these you have pointed out." [22]

In a short preface Twain indicated something of his aim and method by first calling attention to the factual basis for his material and then suggesting that it is capable of universal interpretation:

> Most of the adventures recorded in this book really occurred; one or two were experiences of my own, the rest those of boys who were schoolmates of mine. Huck Finn is drawn from life; Tom Sawyer also, but not from an individual—he is a combination of the characteristics of three boys whom I knew, and therefore belongs to the composite order of architecture.
>
> The odd superstitions touched upon were all prevalent among children and slaves in the West at the period of this story—that is to say, thirty or forty years ago.
>
> Although my book is intended mainly for the entertainment of boys and girls, I hope it will not be shunned by men and women on that account, for part of my plan has been to try to pleasantly remind adults of what they once were themselves, and of how they felt and thought and talked, and what queer enterprises they sometimes engaged in.

Twain announces that his material is to be realistically presented —that is to say, the adventures "really occurred," and the background was founded upon actuality—but, in addition, in his concluding paragraph he suggests that realistic fiction also exists on more than one level of interpretation. Not only is *Tom Sawyer* founded upon fact, but the fact is consciously intended to exist with more universal application. Of course, any literal symbol is capable of universal interpretation, but here one must note that Twain is conscious of the fact and intended that *Tom Sawyer* should, besides entertaining, also serve as a symbol of universal boyhood. Indeed he elsewhere recorded that "Tom Sawyer is simply a hymn, put into prose form to give it a worldly air." [23]

Further evidence that it was Twain's conscious desire to present his material realistically is contained in a letter he addressed to Dr. John Brown of Edinburgh: "But night before last I discovered that that day's Chapter was a failure, in conception, moral truth to nature, and execution—enough blemish to impair the excellence of almost any chapter—and so I must burn up the day's work and do it all over again." [24] Moral truth to nature, not slavish adherence to fact, was an essential of realism for Twain. One must conclude that it was his conscious desire to achieve this realism in *Tom Sawyer*.

But the superiority of *Tom Sawyer* over *The Gilded Age* is not to be accounted for entirely by Twain's sticking to the material he knew best. Part of the excellence of the book must be attributed to the firmer control he exercised over his technique. In the book for boys, he handled his material with a greater degree of objectivity, and thus more artistically, than he had in the earlier satire. He is more often concerned with accurately portraying his subject than he is with telling the reader what to think about it. This firmer control results from his maintaining a consistent narrative point of view by focusing upon Tom without reserving an Olympian attitude for himself as the narrator. Identifying himself with the character of Tom did not allow Twain to make adult judgments directly; to sustain the illusion of reality he had to report on the level of his audience and Tom. Hence, for the most part, his points are made through selection of material and a comment consistent with his narrative viewpoint.

As a result there is little moralizing and a more artful method of letting material speak for itself than Twain customarily employed in his earlier writing. The lapses are few in number—not more than two or three. Such an instance follows the whitewashing of the fence in chapter II. "If he [Tom] had been a great and wise philosopher, like the writer of this book, he would now have comprehended that work consists of whatever a body is obliged to do, and play consists of whatever a body is not obliged to do." [25] Such instances are fortunately rare, much more so than in *The Gilded Age*, where Twain often addresses remarks directly to the reader and even devoted almost an entire chapter to an essay which relieved his feelings but had little to do with the narrative.

Despite Twain's remark about cutting out the satire in *Tom Sawyer*, since the book was to be for boys, a great deal of satire remains; but it is of a different order from that of the earlier work. In *Tom Sawyer* the satire seems more subdued and better integrated with the structure than was true of *The Gilded Age*, wherein the satire was often extraneous and blatant. *Tom Sawyer* is organized about the adventures of Tom, and this chain of adventures over a period of five or six months contributes what unity there is to the novel. Only a few of the adventures, such as the temperance pledge and the Sunday School prize, seem contrived for their satiric intention rather than for any organic relevance to the total effect. In the episode of the graduation exercises, Tom has only a minor role while Twain satirizes at length the puerile sentimentality of schoolgirl compositions. But only these three adventures, among a multitude which crowded Tom's busy summer, seem to offend in this respect.

More often, the barbs of satire are blunted with kindly humor, and the satiric intention of a passage reveals itself subtly rather than overwhelming the reader. Aunt Polly's reaction after Tom's funeral is a case in point. Twain is content to portray the scene dramatically and objectively, allowing it to speak for itself. He does not intrude ironically to direct the reader's attention to the human weakness of curiosity and rationalization of unpleasant facts. Tom confessed that he had been moved to inform his aunt that he was alive by means of a message scratched on a piece of bark, but had not delivered it. Aunt Polly wanted very much to believe that Tom had been actuated by love for her, but was dubious of the truth of his claim; considering Tom's past performance and general disregard for factual accuracy, she had reason to be skeptical.

> The moment he was gone she ran to a closet and got out the ruin of a jacket which Tom had gone pirating in. Then she stopped, with it in her hand, and said to herself: "No, I don't dare. Poor boy, I reckon he's lied about it—but it's a blessed, blessed lie, there's such comfort come from it. I hope the Lord— I know the Lord will forgive him, because it was such goodheartedness in him to tell it. But I don't want to find out it's a lie. I won't look."
> She put the jacket away, and stood by musing a minute. Twice

she put out her hand to take the garment again, and twice she refrained. Once more she ventured, and this time she fortified herself with the thought: "It's a good lie—it's a good lie—I won't let it grieve me." So she sought the jacket pocket. A moment later she was reading Tom's piece of bark through flowing tears and saying: "I could forgive the boy, now if he'd committed a million sins!"

It is an example of the same treatment of material that he tried in "A True Story" and disparages as being out of his line. Pathos underlies the humor of a situation offered without direct comment. It was not conspicuously used in *The Gilded Age*, where the treatment was marked by pointed satire, burlesque, and parody, and where he did not go far beyond the most obvious devices of satire which exaggerate certain aspects of the age rather than depict it realistically. Unlike the earlier work, in *Tom Sawyer* satire is not pushed to the point of caricature.

Tom Sawyer also represents a considerable advance in the formation of Twain's prose style. All the elements previously remarked are abundantly displayed in his first sustained achievement in fiction. The most notable of these qualities are his skillful use of dialect, the easy flow of narrative passages marked by the flavor of good talk, and the apt choice of words to convey his meaning.

Twain does not venture in *Tom Sawyer* the subtle dialect distinctions that were to mark *Huckleberry Finn*. Virtually the only deviation he records is Huck's slightly exaggerated version of the same dialect the rest of the characters speak. He says "hain't" instead of "ain't," for example. The convincing effect of accurate speech is achieved not by distorted spelling but rather by capturing the idiom of the speech he reproduces. In Aunt Polly's soliloquies in the first chapter, for example, Twain alters the spelling of only two words, *spile* instead of *spoil* and *obleeged* instead of *obliged*:

> "Hang the boy, can't I never learn anything? Ain't he played me tricks enough like that for me to be looking out for him by this time? But old fools is the biggest fools there is. Can't learn an old dogs new tricks, as the saying is. But my goodness, he never plays them alike, two days, and how is a body to know what's coming? He 'pears to know just how long he can torment me before I get my dander up, and he knows if he can make out to put me off for a minute or make me laugh, it's all done again

and I can't hit him a lick. . . . Spare the rod and spile the child, as the Good Book says. . . . He's full of the Old Scratch, but laws-a-me! he's my own dead sister's boy, poor thing, and I ain't got the heart to lash him, somehow. . . . Well-a well, man that is born of woman is of few days and full of trouble, as the Scripture says, and I reckon it's so. He'll play hookey this evening,* [* South-western for 'afternoon.' (Twain's note)] and I'll just be obleeged to make him work, tomorrow, to punish him."

When Twain had attempted dialect in *The Gilded Age*, he had been closer to the Southwest humor tradition of exaggerated spelling. Compare, for example, the following comments of Old Damrell, one of the Obedstown characters:

Ole Drake Higgens he's ben down to Shelby las' week. Tuck his crap down; couldn't git shet o' the most uv it; hit warn't no time for to sell, he say, so he fotch it back agin, 'lowin' to wait tell fall. Talks 'bout goin' to Mosouri—lots uv' ems talkin' that-away down thar, Ole Higgens say.

The point to be made here is that in abandoning the attempt to capture the literal sound of speech and striving instead to achieve the flavor of it through idiom and syntax, Twain arrived at a more artful employment of dialect in *Tom Sawyer* than he had yet reached.

Likewise, the narrative portions of the book are highly colored by the rhythm of speech. A random example will illustrate the oral character of the prose:

He bravely bore his miseries three weeks, and then one day turned up missing. For forty-eight hours the widow hunted for him everywhere in great distress. The public were profoundly concerned; they searched high and low, they dragged the river for his body. Early the third morning Tom Sawyer wisely went poking among some old empty hogsheads down behind the abandoned slaughter-house, and in one of them he found the refugee. Huck had slept there; he had just breakfasted upon some stolen odds and ends of food, and was lying off, now, in comfort, with his pipe. He was unkempt, uncombed, and clad in the same old ruin of rags that had made him picturesque in the days when he was free and happy. Tom routed him out, told him the trouble he had been causing, and urged him to go home. Huck's face lost its tranquil content, and took a melancholy cast.

Two qualities point to the unmistakably oral flavor of this prose. The first is the number of alliterating pairs of words. There are seven instances in the passage: *bravely bore, for forty-eight, public-profoundly, the third, wisely went, unkempt uncombed,* and *ruin rags.* The word *unkempt* deserves particular notice. It is an exact synonym for *uncombed,* and the sense of the phrase would suggest that *unkept* would have been a more logical choice. One is forced to conclude that repetition of sound must have been an important factor in the choice Twain made. This fondness for alliterating pairs is highly characteristic of Twain's prose throughout his mature writing.

The second aspect of the passage pointing to Twain's playing by ear is the consonantal pattern. As one closely examines the selection, he may note how a dominant sound tends to be repeated until supplanted by another which, in turn, is repeated. The passage opens with *b* dominant, but coupled with *r* in *bravely bore.* The letter *b* is relatively rare in commonly used words; therefore the *r* sound predominates in the following words for a third of the passage: *miseries, three, turned, for, forty-eight, hours, for, everywhere, great, distress, profoundly, concerned, searched, dragged, river, early, third, morning.* The heavily accented *b*'s, however, reassert themselves as labials, first as *p* in *public, profoundly, poked,* and then modified to *f* in *found, refugee, breakfasted, food,* and *comfort.* In this middle third of labials gradually supplanting the *r,* the sound of hard *c* has obtruded in *poking, Huck, breakfasted,* and *comfort.* The sound is heavily underscored by the words *unkempt* and *uncombed.* Thereafter, in the last third, the hard *c* modified by *t* predominates in *clad, picturesque, routed, out, told, trouble, causing, tranquil, content, took, melancholy, cast.* The passage may be described in terms of sound value almost as though it were a piece of music. This dependence upon sound is inherent in all of Twain's prose and must be taken into account as one of the important qualities of what is generally regarded as one of the distinguished prose styles in American literature. It, just as the other qualities noted, entered into the creation of *Tom Sawyer* as the first independent, extended display of Twain's talent in fiction; and it, as well as the other elements of Twain's craft, was to be even more notable in *Huckleberry Finn* and never entirely thereafter abandoned in the rest of his work.

V

The Craft of
Huckleberry Finn

HUCKLEBERRY FINN provides the most impressive display of Twain's craft. It is raised above the level of his other novels, partly because his style is more richly informed by a moral viewpoint that invests the events he related with some universal purpose beyond that of entertainment alone.

Twain's material was not radically different from that of *The Gilded Age* or *Tom Sawyer*. The same setting and essentially the same people still concern him. The difference lies in the fact that his material is more significantly informed by the assumptions upon which his style is founded. These assumptions are largely moral and philosophical ones concerning the nature of man and his relation to his fellow man. In short, his material is treated more significantly because it is ordered upon an underlying framework of belief about important aspects of the nature of man.

The source of his belief was in his experience, and his early experience was among the folk, pre-eminently concerned with the moral nature of reality. In *Huckleberry Finn*, to a greater extent than before, Twain as an artist was the spokesman of the folk dealing in common sense much admired by the folk, while at the same time picturing essentially primitive mentalities at work using a mixture of common sense and superstition to cope with their problems.

By contrast, the dominant view of *Tom Sawyer* was that of boyhood rather than of the folk. To some extent the latter view is displayed by Aunt Polly as well as secondarily by other characters, but not as significantly as in *Huckleberry Finn*. Among such people the elements of good and bad luck play an important role in their daily lives. But luck is not entirely a matter of chance; it is rather a moral state related to one's behavior. Good or bad luck is the outcome of one's actions. Man moves in a world full of ominous signs and portents; he must be constantly alert to ward off evil and must cultivate certain ritualistic practices to encourage good consequences. Huck recounts one of numerous such situations pervading his adventure in chapter I:

> Pretty soon a spider went crawling up my shoulder, and I flipped it off and it lit in the candle; and before I could budge it was all shriveled up. I didn't need anybody to tell me that that was an awful bad sign and would fetch me some bad luck, so I was scared and most shook the clothes off of me. I got up and turned around in my tracks three times and crossed my breast every time; and then I tied up a little lock of my hair with a thread to keep witches away.

Moral choice rests not alone in remote and mysterious areas of man's life, but his real, everyday world, over which he exercises considerable control, is circumscribed by moral issues to be resolved. Huck chooses to lie often, but is culpable only when he wantonly lies to Jim. He ironically chooses to go to hell. He reports the moral choices others make. And in each instance it is the problem of the moral nature of reality that underlies the resolution of the incident. It is this preoccupation with a most important aspect of mankind's concerns that gives *Huckleberry Finn* added substance and significance as a display of Twain's art. He has plunged beneath the surface texture of his experience and dealt with moral assumptions forming the basis of his belief about his experience.

There is scarcely an episode, character, or place in *Huckleberry Finn* that was not closely associated with Twain's personal experience. Every inch of land and water covered by Huck had been traveled countless times by Twain. Many of the characters, according to numerous statements Twain made, were based upon specific individuals; and all the other characters, according to DeVoto's *Mark Twain's America*, had their counterparts in types who flourished on the river and must have been observed by

Twain as a small boy in Hannibal and later during his days as a pilot on the river. In no instance does Twain depart from the physical and social aspects of a life he had known intimately and almost daily from his early boyhood through his years as a cub pilot. No one can carp or quibble over the authenticity of the image of a society captured by Twain in *Huckleberry Finn*.

The book also reveals the maturation of one of the finest prose styles in American literature. All the elements of Twain's style came to their full fruition in this work, and, although there were to be later occasions on which Twain partly repeated his achievement in *Huckleberry Finn*, there was never to be a sustained effort to match this earlier one.

The same photographic quality of Twain's handling of scenes in *Tom Sawyer* also marks *Huckleberry Finn*, but with an important difference. Where many episodes of the earlier work were static and two-dimensionally pictorial, in the second there is a change toward a more dynamic handling of the episodes. There is more vitality and movement; the characters make gestures, change their positions, and do things as they talk more often than was true of the earlier novels.

Part of this difference must be attributed to the happy device of the first person narration, for it does not allow Twain to depart from the experience of his narrator. Obviously a more realistic effect of verisimilitude is achieved by its use, but the device also has a subtle effect upon Twain's style. The viewpoint brings the reader closer to the events than would an impersonal and more objective omniscient narrative point of view. The reader is in the midst of the action rather than in the posture of a detached observer, and thus is achieved the illusion of greater activity surrounding the reader.

But at the same time, Huck's own view, with which the reader identifies himself, is not openly partisan. He simply records what he observes and makes sparing comment upon it, as for the moment the reader is willing to accept his fresh, unsophisticated view of the life he observes. Not until he has finished the book is the reader likely to reflect that there was an intelligence behind Huck's selecting what he stated. The book fairly lives and breathes; it is quick with the substance of life itself. It penetrates the surface appearance of the life it records and goes directly to the inner reality in the moral issue it illuminates.

This three-dimensional quality of life itself, rather than a mere picture of life, is achieved partly by a greater degree of sensory imagery than Twain had heretofore used. The whitewashing-of-the-fence scene in *Tom Sawyer* was composed entirely of visual images and dialogue, but in *Huckleberry Finn* there are more auditory, olfactory, and tactile images. Huck hears the k'chunk of an ax chopping wood long after the blow was struck across the water. He attempts to render sensorily the effect of a storm when he reports, "then comes a *h-whack-bum!* bum! bumble-umble-um-bum-bum-bum-bum and the thunder would go rumbling and grumbling away, and quit—and then *rip* comes another flash and another sockdolager."

In addition to the imagery, another element in Twain's style that reinforces its lifelike effect is the wealth of specific detail. Huck names each item of treasure he and Jim rescue from the house of death; even the most trivial one is described with often no more than a word or two that renders it a unique specimen among its class. They find not just a few old bottles of medicine, but "some vials of medicine that didn't have no label on them." One discarded item is a baby's nursing bottle, but it is not reported as an example of a class of objects. Instead of calling it a baby's nursing bottle, which would be a reasoned conclusion from its appearance, he more objectively describes its properties: ". . . there was a bottle that had milk in it, and it had a rag stopper for a baby to suck. We would'a' took the bottle, but it was broke." And later, describing the furnishings in the house of the Granger-fords, Twain must list the title of each book. Of course, there is a bit of humor involved in each instance, but the use of specific detail results in a more convincing air of actuality.

Closely related to the foregoing aspects of style is the highly colloquial flavor of Twain's prose. In *Huckleberry Finn* the first person narrative viewpoint accounts for the necessity of a language in keeping with Huck's character, but this fact alone does not justify Twain's obviously close attention to spoken language. In a short preface he comments upon the various dialects employed.

In this book a number of dialects are used, to wit: the Missouri negro dialect; the extremest form of the backwoods Southwestern dialect; the ordinary "Pike County" dialect; and four modified varieties of this last. The shadings have not been done in a haphazard fashion, or by guesswork; but painstakingly, and with the trustworthy guidance and support of personal familiarity with these several forms of speech.

Twain was always interested in the spoken language; his work throughout his life reflected it, and even the most prosaic observation he might make was likely to be enlivened by the informality and aptness of its colloquial expression.

Huckleberry Finn has often been regarded as one of the few instances in which a sequel has reached or surpassed the success of its predecessor. But it is only a sequel in the sense that it was written after *Tom Sawyer* and made use of some of the same characters and setting. The implication of the term that the second work continues the themes and further exploits the methods and excellences of the first is not realized in this instance. Though in the first four chapters there is the intention to continue the story and further adventures of Tom Sawyer, the book departs from its model and, in spite of superficial similarities, becomes a profoundly different story. One difference is the addition of greater moral significance to *Huckleberry Finn;* also, Twain exhibits greater narrative skill and more successfully applies his principles of composition.

Huckleberry Finn was written entirely in accord with his consciously professed ideas of narration. These notions have already been examined at some length, but, in brief, Twain regarded his function as the objective reporting in realistic style of a narrative which he had merely set in motion. One of several attempts to describe the process may be found in *Mark Twain in Eruption*:

> Experience has taught me long ago that if I tell a boy's story, or anybody else's, it is never worth printing; it comes from the head not the heart, and always goes into the wastebasket. To be successful and worth printing, the imagined boy would have to tell his story himself and let me act merely as his amanuensis. . . . When a tale tells itself there is no trouble about it; there are no hesitancies, no delays, no cogitations, no attempts at invention; there is nothing to do but hold the pen and let the story talk through it and say, after its own fashion, what it desires to say.[1]

The method is not as anarchical as it might at first appear. Twain did not mean that first person narration was best, though this was the narrative point of view of *Huckleberry Finn*. What he seems to be describing is the logic that links event to event as in actual life. An episode does not have to be invented; it should be produced by the intersection of antecedent character and situation. Once it takes place a new situation exists, and the consequent impact of it upon character produces another situation. There is a continuous flow of event logically following event. Success in capturing this flow depends upon not only the author's ability at sustaining his characters but also his experience with observing human motivation. Thus the story appears to unfold without interference on the part of the writer; however, consciously or unconsciously, the writer does control the direction of flow of these events. The control is informed by the author's experience, whether consciously or intuitively apprehended and assimilated, which serves as the norm by which he selects and values his material. Twain seems consciously to have espoused a method that applied principles unconsciously, with the author under the delusion that it involved no principles at all. A statement he made in connection with the dictation of his autobiography makes the point clear:

> With the pen in one's hand, narrative is a difficult art; narrative should flow as flows the brook down through the hills and the leafy woodlands, its course changed by every boulder it comes across and by every grass-clad gravelly spur that projects into its path; its surface broken, but its course not stayed by rocks and gravel on the bottom in the shoal places; a brook that never goes straight for a minute, but *goes*, and goes briskly, sometimes ungrammatically, and sometimes fetching a horseshoe three-quarters of a mile around, and at the end of the circuit flowing within a yard of the path it traversed an hour before; but always *going*, and always following at least one law, always loyal to that law, the law of *narrative*, which *has no law*.[2]

Twain's paradoxical conclusion was uttered probably for rhetorical effect rather than out of sincere conviction. Of course, there are "laws" and principles of narration. The aimlessness of the brook in Twain's example is only apparent; it obeys the elementary physical law that water seeks the lowest level. And successful narrative fiction obeys its own principles inherent in the experience it records and selected by the norms of its narrator whether he is conscious of the fact or not. In his best work Twain seems to have followed this method: consciously he created his characters and treated them and the situations involving them realistically, but what happened to them was not consciously his affair; they acted out their story controlled only by Twain's intuitive selection of event, which—fortunately in most instances—was conditioned by his prejudice in favor of realism, allowing the plot to develop logically, if erratically. When he contrived plot and situation in advance, however, he fell into difficulty trying to create appropriate characters and force them to obey the demands of plot. Such was the case with Laura in *The Gilded Age*. Happily, for the most part the method worked in *Huckleberry Finn*. Though one cannot claim it is the best method to tell a story, it seems to have been the most fruitful for Twain and perhaps accounts for the reason why his achievement was to remain uneven—even within his greatest work.

Understanding this semiconscious method of narration, one must take with a grain of salt Twain's injunction in his prefatory notice to *Huckleberry Finn*: "Persons attempting to find a motive in this narrative will be prosecuted; persons attempting to find a moral in it will be banished; persons attempting to find a plot in it will be shot." Of course there are motive, moral, and plot in the book, but of a quite different order from *The Prince and the Pauper*, which was published before *Huckleberry Finn* was completed. The former book was motivated by Twain's dislike for monarchy and social evil resulting from monarchical abuse; in it Twain moralized upon the quality of mercy, taking from *The Merchant of Venice* his thesis that mercy "becomes the throned monarch better than his crown." And the plot of the prince and his poor double trading places was fabricated in advance. In the sense that motive, moral, and plot are used in *The Prince and the Pauper*, Twain's disclaimer in *Huckleberry Finn* is tenable. He does not write to a thesis nor conform to a preconceived plot structure. But, since *Huckleberry Finn* was thought of by Twain as a sequel to *Tom Sawyer*, one may assume that a measure of the intention of *Tom Sawyer* is probably also true of *Huckle-*

berry Finn. The book was intended not only for the entertainment of boys and girls, but also to remind adults of their own youth. In other words, Twain wanted it to have a limited symbolic significance.

If motive, moral, and plot were not consciously intended by Twain as they were in *The Prince and the Pauper,* they are nevertheless significantly present in *Huckleberry Finn* as the product of Twain's unconscious cerebration operating in company with his method of letting his story tell itself; they are inherent in the very material he selects and arranges. The plot in any work of fiction carries the chief burden of statement; it embraces all other elements of the narrative and gives them some structure and meaning as they are focused toward the outcome of events. Not all plots achieve this end, and in such instances we speak of absence of plot or looseness and lack of unity; this is the accusation that has usually been made against *Tom Sawyer* and *Huckleberry Finn.* There are grounds for the assertion, but it gives a misleading idea of Twain's increasing narrative skill to imply that there is no difference in this respect between the two companion pieces.

The plot is regarded as picaresque, and critical attention has been called to the resemblances between *Huckleberry Finn* and *Don Quixote.* Unfortunately, this essentially just comparison can be misleading because of the implications of the term *picaresque.* Its use denominates a plot as a series of relatively unrelated adventures held together by its central character, usually a rogue, and perhaps by a common motif, as with *Don Quixote.* But the plot lacks the unity which would find meaning in the relationship of succeeding events. The events of a picaresque novel are arranged chronologically, but without other relationship; any given adventure might as well take place at the beginning as toward the end of the narrative. Obviously, character in such a plot must be static. Little character development can take place, for if it does, events must assume a necessary logical order, and unity results.

In this light it is proper to regard the plot of *Tom Sawyer* as picaresque, but *Huckleberry Finn* is an advance over *Tom Sawyer.* The picaresque elements are superficial, if more striking, and a measure of unity is achieved that was not true of *Tom Sawyer.*

Unlike Tom the romantic, Huck himself always keeps in close touch with actuality. With the assurance of a seemingly uncomplex personality, he has the faculty of dispelling clouds of illusion by breezy puffs of simple, naive reason. His logic may bring a smile to more sophisticated thinkers, but his conclusions are disturbing because they do ignore nonessentials and plunge directly to the heart of matters. The narrative point of view perforce must reflect the more realistic attitude of Huck, and since he unfolds his own story, the plot is also more realistic. It captures the flow of event following event with fidelity to the probability of human experience; it mirrors the same logic that seems to operate in actual life when one event precipitates the next with the inevitability of a syllogism. Thus the plot of *Huckleberry Finn* differs from and marks an artistic advance over *Tom Sawyer*. In the earlier work there was no necessary relationship of the various adventures. Twain's theme was the universal one of boyhood, with Tom as its chief symbol; it was illustrated by a collection of adventures concerning the queer enterprises boys sometimes engaged in. And it does not matter in what order the adventures occurred. Tom might as well have whitewashed his fence at the end of that crowded summer as at the beginning so far as the episode has anything to do with his character development.

But generally the same statement cannot be made of *Huckleberry Finn*. In a greater measure a logical sequence of events is observed, and what holds the incidents together and provides the continuity of movement is Twain's motivating moral theme. It is one of freedom and escape, actually two aspects of a single fundamental moral issue. He asks how the individual can remain free in a restrictive society and answers that he is compelled to flee; morally he does right by doing wrong. The morally right society from which Huck flees is mainly characterized by man's inhumanity to man, and the morally wrong society created on the raft demonstrates man's potential for nobility of character in the relationship between Huck and Jim. In the process of gaining his freedom, Huck learns that he must assume moral responsibility for his actions.

The first three chapters link the story of Tom Sawyer as

though it were to continue the earlier adventures. Tom Sawyer's gang is organized with appropriate solemn oaths and then languishes until Tom rallies his forces to attack the "A-rabs." But an air of disillusion hangs over the adventure; Huck is not deluded by Tom's romantic lies. His practical, realistic view is the source of the new ironic humor of these adventures. Tom said that magicians had turned the soldiers, elephants, and treasure into an infant Sunday School. "I said, all right; then the thing for us to do was to go for the magicians. Tom Sawyer said I was a numskull." The adventures cannot continue in the carefree fashion of those of the earlier book; there is in the early chapter the premonition of more serious events to come. Huck inadvertently kills a spider in the first chapter, and he knows of no way to forestall the consequent bad luck. Later he spills salt at breakfast and is prevented by Miss Watson from warding off bad luck. Jim's hair-ball is not reassuring, and Pap Finn does return to kidnap and terrorize Huck.

After Pap's drunken struggle with the Death Angel, the independent waif realizes his life is in danger, and he must flee. To forestall pursuit he must appear to be dead; it is the only way he can sever the bonds of the moral and physical slavery of his life in St. Petersburg. Miss Watson represents the stifling forces of "sivilization," his father the brutal oppression of ignorance. "Sivilization" seems to Huck a narrow life composed of proscriptions against everything pleasurable. There are no tangible rewards, and the path of virtue leads to a dull heaven. The free and easy existence with his father in the woods was a better choice. "I didn't want to go back to the widow's any more and be so cramped and sivilized, as they called it." But the drunken Pap soon proves to be not much better. Before getting drunk he excoriates the "govment" that lets a nigger run free and even vote! "I says I'll never vote ag'in. Them's the very words I said; they all heard me; and the country may rot for all of me—I'll never vote ag'in as long as I live. And to see the cool way of that nigger—why, he wouldn't a give me the road if I hadn't shoved him out o' the way." Pap is the prototype of all the jurymen Twain would have us believe this country could supply. "The jury system puts a ban upon intelligence and honesty, and a premium upon ignorance, stupidity and perjury." ³ Huck at first thought of striking out across country, living off the land until he was out of reach of Pap and the Widow Douglas, but arranging the scene to make it appear that he had been murdered was better; it forestalled pursuit from the start and allowed him to laze on Jackson Island and enjoy the spectacle as the "pirates" had done before in *Tom Sawyer*.

When Huck is joined by the fugitive Jim and the odyssey down the river is begun, the divergence from the adventures in *Tom Sawyer* is complete. The scope of the story is widened. No longer confined to village boy's life, Huck moves in an adult world and brings his realistic view to bear upon that world more significantly than upon the childish, romantic one of Tom. But even Jackson Island is too close to "sivilization," and Huck and Jim transfer to another island—the raft—which floats free upon the water. On the raft the two fugitives create a society of their own. Generally Huck bows to Jim's superior wisdom because it is confirmed by Huck's own experience. They discuss whether stars were made or just happened. "Jim said the moon could'a *laid* them; well, that looked kind of reasonable, so I didn't say nothing against it, because I've seen a frog lay most as many, so of course it could be done." From Jim, Huck learns humility. "It was fifteen minutes before I could work myself up to go and humble myself to a nigger; but I done it, and I warn't ever sorry for it afterwards, neither." His only reward is Jim's trust: "Dah you goes, de ole true Huck; de on'y white genlman dat ever kep' his promise to old Jim." It is enough to keep Huck on the path of "wrong" in helping Jim escape. Numerous times Huck pays tribute to the life they lead. "We said there warn't no home like a raft, after all. Other places do seem so cramped up and smothery, but a raft don't. You feel mighty free and easy and comfortable on a raft." And later he says, "It's lovely to live on a raft."

The raft frequently comes in contact with more "sivilized" forms of life on shore. Each such contact is a variation of the "niceness" or brutality from which Jim and Huck flee, a further illustration of the irrational codes by which men live in villages. Huck does not moralize about what he observes, but the contrast with the life on the raft is obvious.

After witnessing the violent conclusion of the Grangerford-

Shepherdson feud, Huck says, "I ain't a-going to tell *all* that happened—it would make me sick again if I was to do that. I wished I hadn't ever come ashore that night to see such things. I ain't ever going to get shut of them—lots of times I dream about them." It is the way of feuds in real life; lovers can unite the two families only in romance. Twain deliberately intended to parody the romantic representation of feuding. After recounting Emmeline Grangerford's sentimental drawing and poetry, Huck listens to Buck define a feud:

> "Well," says Buck, "a feud is this way: A man has a quarrel with another man, and kills him; then that other man's brother kills him: then the other brothers, on both sides, goes for one another; then the cousins chip in—and by and by everybody's killed off, and there ain't no more feud. But it's kind of slow, and takes a long time."

The Duke and the Dauphin come aboard, and Huck realistically accepts them:

> It didn't take me long to make up my mind that these liars warn't no kings nor dukes at all, but just low-down humbugs and frauds. But I never said nothing, never let on; kept it to myself; it's the best way; then you don't have no quarrels, and don't get into no trouble. If they wanted us to call them kings and dukes, I hadn't no objection, 'long as it would keep peace in the family, and it warn't no use to tell Jim, so I didn't tell him. If I never learnt nothing else out of Pap, I learnt that the best way to get along with his kind of people is to let them have their own way.

And again when Huck witnesses the cowardice of the mob that failed to lynch Colonel Sherburn, he says,

> Sherburn run his eye slow along the crowd; and wherever it struck the people tried a little to outgaze him, but they couldn't; they dropped their eyes and looked sneaky. . . . The crowd washed back sudden, and then broke all apart, and went tearing off every which way; and Buck Harkness he heeled it after them, looking tolerable cheap. I could 'a' stayed if I wanted to, but I didn't want to.

Huck is a camera's eye, recording the motion of events on which it is trained. But Huck is something more. He has learned to be a morally responsible human being who can make an independent decision dictated by what he knows to be right. "Then I'll go to hell," he decides as he chooses to help Jim escape, and thus he elevates himself to symbolize the fundamental bias toward good which motivates the best of mankind. And when he stands squarely on his own feet and assumes responsibility for a moral choice dictated by what he feels to be right instead of shifting responsibility to a choice rationalized by morally irresponsible codes of behavior, Huck gains the dignity and nobility of which mankind is capable.

The lesson Huck demonstrates is the moral key to the problem of man's inhumanity to man. A man realizes freedom and manhood only when he assumes moral responsibility for his conduct. Any other view, which denies that man is his own moral agent, robs mankind of its humanity. It tends to a mechanistic view of man and dehumanizes him. Dehumanized men are inevitably inhumane to one another.

When Huck reaches the Phelps's farm, he has earned his freedom and manhood through his experiences on the river and from Jim as his guide and tutor. The farcical conclusion of Jim's escape engineered by Tom, in the light of the moral theme developed to this point, is not as pointlessly anticlimactic as critics have usually held. It is not a mere appendage, but is ironically related to the preceding events. Huck loses some of his earlier stature in this later role as a foil to Tom, but he still breathes cool common sense over Tom's hot romanticism. Huck's presence and Jim's simple dignity in standing by when Tom was shot make Tom's puerile shenanigans all the more obviously morally irresponsible, and even inhumane after we learn that Tom knew all along that Jim had been given his freedom. This concluding episode is most unflattering to Tom and rightly offends the reader's sense of fitness and decorum. Following upon the odyssey down the river, the conclusion appears to be only anticlimactic, the tomfoolery to be only childish and irresponsible. But upon reflection one must also conclude that Tom's code of behavior is fundamentally no more childishly romantic and irresponsible than were the codes that Huck observed operating in St. Petersburg and the various villages down the river.

The source of Tom's ethics was in books, and, of course, this accounts for the inanity of behavior based thereupon, for a social code based upon romantic "lying books" will not withstand the test of common sense. The point is established early in the story when Ben Rogers asks Tom how the gang is to go about ransoming prisoners. Tom is at a loss for an answer, but doggedly sticks to his models of behavior.

"I don't know. But that's what they do. I've seen it in books; and so of course that's what we've got to do."

"But how can we do it if we don't know what it is?"

"Why, blame it all, we've *got* to do it. Don't I tell you it's in the books? Do you want to go to doing different from what's in the books, and get things all muddled up?"

"Oh, that's all very fine to *say*, Tom Sawyer, but how in the nation are these fellows going to be ransomed if we don't know how to do it to them? . . .

"Well, I don't know. But per'aps if we keep them till they're dead."

". . . and a bothersome lot they'll be, too—eating up everything, and always trying to get loose . . . why can't a body take a club and ransom them as soon as they get here?"

"Because it ain't in the books so—that's why. Now, Ben Rogers, do you want to do things regular, or don't you?—that's the idea. Don't you reckon that the people that made the books know what's the correct thing to do? Do you reckon you can learn 'em anything? Not by a good deal."

The unconscious irony of Tom's last speech should be obvious. Tom uncritically subscribes to the forms of an alien culture. In a similar fashion each stratum of society upon which Huck reports pins its faith on certain forms and rituals and draws its morality from them. Miss Watson's code, to which Huck must conform, is drawn from the Old Testament, the legacy of an archaic Hebrew culture, and the Widow Douglas would equip the ragamuffin with the social graces of a Virginia gentleman. "Don't put your feet up there, Huckleberry"; and "Don't scrunch up like that, Huckleberry—why don't you try to behave?"

Further evidence that it was Twain's intention deliberately to examine such codes of ethics is suggested by his treatment of criminal behavior. One of the robbers on the *Walter Scott* proposes to dispose of an unreliable colleague by permitting him to drown. "He'll be drownded, and won't have nobody to blame for it but his own self. I reckon that's a considerable sight better'n killin' of him. I'm unfavorable to killin' a man as long as you can git aroun' it, it ain't good sense, it ain't good morals."

The Duke and the King are of the same stripe, but their pretensions to nobility make them, as well as the institutions of aristocracy, ridiculous. Just as absurd is the conduct of the Grangerford-Shepherdson feud according to the laws of the frontier aristocracy. "Colonel Grangerford was a gentleman, you see. He was a gentleman all over; and so was his family." What the code of the gentleman entailed Twain described elsewhere:

> In Missouri a recognized superiority attached to any person who hailed from Old Virginia. . . . The F.F.V. was born a gentleman; his highest duty in life was to watch over that great inheritance and keep it unsmirched. He must keep his honor spotless. Those laws were his chart; his course was marked out on it. . . . These laws required certain things of him which his religion might forbid: then his religion must yield—the laws could not be relaxed to accommodate religions or anything else.[4]

In contrast to such an ideal, Sherburn faces up to the mob that comes to lynch him and praises the rare *man* as opposed to the mob. "Why, a *man's* safe in the hands of ten thousand of your kind. . . ." In castigating the mob Sherburn emphasizes the word *man* by constant repetition; sixteen times in his speech he repeats the word, six times it being italicized for emphasis. He lauds a code of physical courage as opposed to cowardice, and with his manly courage he routs the mob singlehanded. The meaning of the passage, however, is not so much to affirm a code of manliness as it is to demonstrate Twain's conviction that the average man lacks courage, and in a mob, lest his cowardice be found out, he accepts through fear a code of behavior imposed by a leader.

> Your newspapers call you a brave people so much that you think you *are* braver than any other people—whereas you're just *as* brave, and no braver. Why don't your juries hang murderers? Because they're afraid the man's friends will shoot them in the back, in the dark. . . . The average man don't like trouble and danger. . . . The pitifulest thing out is a mob; that's what an army is—a mob; they don't fight with courage that's born in them, but with courage that's borrowed from their mass, and

from their officers. But a mob without any *man* at the head of it is *beneath* pitifulness.

The ethical codes of Huck and Jim, however, differ in that they are neither lifted from an alien social context nor followed blindly. In a sense their social behavior is more rational in that it is indigenous, the product of their native heritage; application of their moral ideals in practical life is based both on firsthand observation of society and common-sense analysis of their experience. Of course, outside their range of experience and rational ability they must depend upon the native rituals of superstition for explanation and control of phenomena, but within their accustomed sphere they work out their moral problems reasonably and humanely and achieve a measure of the dignity possible for man.

This folk common-sense morality is not confined to Jim and Huck alone. Mrs. Judith Loftus, for example, exhibits a share of it when she shrewdly penetrates Huck's disguise as a girl, but nonetheless aids him in his deception. It is Jim and Huck, however, who consistently keep these folk values before the reader, nor does Twain obtrude them obviously. They arise logically out of situations as naturally as Huck breathes. The Widow, for example, tries to "learn" Huck about "Moses and the Bulrushers," but Huck "don't take no stock in dead people."

> Pretty soon I wanted to smoke, and asked the widow to let me. But she wouldn't. She said it was a mean practice and wasn't clean, and I must try to not do it any more. That is just the way with some people. They get down on a thing when they don't know nothing about it. Here she was abothering about Moses, which was no kin to her, and no use to anybody, being gone, you see, yet finding a power of fault with me for doing a thing that had some good in it. And she took snuff, too; of course, that was all right, because she done it herself.

Huck shrewdly observes the operation of a double standard of morality, and in warding off intruders with a lie about smallpox being on board the raft, he no less shrewdly judges the self-interest motivating most moral behavior. But in analyzing his own motives dictating his moral choice in this situation, he is disturbed by his moral conclusion:

They went off and I got aboard the raft, feeling bad and low, because I knowed very well I had done wrong, and I see it warn't no use for me to try to learn to do right. . . . Then I thought a minute, and says to myself, hold on; s'pose you'd 'a' done right and give Jim up, would you felt better than what you do now? No, says I, I'd feel bad—I'd feel just the same way I do now. Well, then, says I what's the use you learning to do right when it's troublesome to do right and ain't no trouble to do wrong, and the wages is just the same?

Jim is no less shrewd in his application of common-sense morality. He is unimpressed by Huck's recital of Solomon's vaunted wisdom.

. . . de man dat think he kin settle a 'spute 'bout a whole chile wid a half a chile doan' know enough to come in out'n de rain. . . . It lays in de way Sollermun was raised. You take a man dat's got on'y one or two chillen; is dat man gwyne to be waseful o' chillen? No, he ain't; he can't 'ford it. *He* knows how to value 'em.

Jim recognizes when he has performed an inhumane act, as when he punished his daughter before discovering she was deaf and dumb. And from Jim's moral wisdom and humanity, Huck learns the moral responsibility of friendship. Jim says, "Trash is what people is dat puts dirt on de head er dey fren's en makes 'em ashamed." Huck reports that "It was fifteen minutes before I could work myself up to go and humble myself to a nigger; but I done it, and I warn't ever sorry for it afterward, neither."

In the moral theme developed throughout *Huckleberry Finn*, Twain has informed his work more positively with a set of values drawn from his experience with the folk than was true in *Tom Sawyer*. The superiority of *Huckleberry Finn* over the earlier book lies not alone in a more skillful exercise of Twain's craft, but in that his craft is also inextricably linked with greater moral significance. It is one of the most significant examinations in American literature of the codes by which men live. And Huck in his last words of the book keeps the fact before the reader's mind: "Aunt Sally she's going to adopt me and sivilize me, and I can't stand it. I been there before."

VI

A Connecticut Yankee and *The Prince and the Pauper:* Structure and Meaning

To SOME EXTENT Twain departs from his principles of realism in *A Connecticut Yankee*, and in its closely related predecessor *The Prince and the Pauper*, chiefly as a consequence of the propaganda purpose of these novels. Both books are too weighted with sociocritical ideas to be entirely satisfying as novels. *Huckleberry Finn* was critical of the society it portrayed, but in that instance the ideas seem to have grown logically out of the material examined, whereas *The Prince and the Pauper* and *A Connecticut Yankee* give the impression that the material was selected to illustrate a thesis.

The writer, of course, approaches the composition of any work with a body of beliefs which he holds, but the process of writing is also one of discovery. It is now generally a critical commonplace to observe that, as he writes, the novelist gradually learns what his story is, and not until it is quite complete does he really discover his story. Moreover, this discovery does not necessarily suggest the author's complete awareness. *Huckleberry Finn* seems to have been composed somewhat after this fashion, but in the writing of *The Prince and the Pauper* and *A Connecticut Yankee*, Twain thought he knew in advance what he wanted his stories to be. They do not unfold themselves to the reader as does

Huckleberry Finn, but rather marshall themselves as evidence to prove a point. But this is not to say that they are logically and coherently organized about a central issue, for in organization they are typical of Twain's discursive approach. However, a rough unity of purpose is discernible within them that does accord them some measure of design beyond Twain's customary achievement.

The Prince and the Pauper was published in December, 1881, before *Huckleberry Finn,* because, although the latter was begun almost immediately after the publication of *Tom Sawyer* in 1876, Twain's "tank ran dry," and *Huckleberry Finn* was shelved for several years before Twain returned to it and completed the book in 1883. *The Prince and the Pauper* was begun in the summer of 1877; it too was shelved for a time, but was taken up with *Huckleberry Finn* again in 1880, and then Twain alternately worked on them both, completing *The Prince and the Pauper* first.

Twain outlined the plot with more care than was his custom in order to keep the story within the limits of historical fact and to illustrate his thesis. Because he was forced to stay within the historical time between the death of Henry VIII and the prince's coronation, he could not take the discursive liberties of *Tom Sawyer* and *Huckleberry Finn;* moreover, his thesis controlled the kind of events he could select or invent as relevant to his purpose. As a consequence he produced a plot unified in the conventional sense understood by the novel-reading audience of his time.

The plot hinges upon a variation of the twin theme—a constantly recurring motif for Twain. Two look-alikes trade places. One is Tom Canty, a slum-dwelling boy raised in a blighted area of London; the other is the young prince, later to become Edward VI. The story alternates between Tom's uneasy masquerade as a young monarch almost to the moment of his coronation and the picaresque adventure of the young king. The latter plot gets the greater emphasis. In company with a dispossessed nobleman as his protector, the king is subjected to a series of episodes in which he is regarded as mentally deranged. During this revealing experience, the prince learns a great deal about his subjects and their sufferings under oppressive laws and economic exploitation.

The book was acclaimed as a newer and higher achievement than any of his previous fiction. Certainly his earlier misgivings about its reception were dispelled. He had told Mrs. A. W. Fairbanks that it would appear without his name, "such grave and stately work being considered by the world to be above my proper level." [1] His wife and Howells both assured him that it should appear as his own work; indeed, Olivia was more enthusiastic about this book than any other Twain had produced. Her critical judgment would seem to have been vindicated by the success of *The Prince and the Pauper,* but it should not be surprising. Her tastes reflected her upbringing, and they were those of conventionally accepted standards of the day. *The Prince and the Pauper* more than any of Twain's earlier works met those standards and consequently was judged more successful, meeting with greater critical and popular favor than either *Tom Sawyer* or *Huckleberry Finn,* though it did not match the commercial success of his earlier books.

To Howells in March, 1880, Twain described what he felt to be the controlling purpose of his tale in *The Prince and the Pauper:*

> My idea is to afford a realizing sense of the exceeding severity of the laws of the day by inflicting some of their penalties upon the king himself and allowing him a chance to see the rest of them applied to others—all of which is to account for certain mildnesses which distinguished Edward VI's reign from those that preceded and followed it. [2]

Twain took the text for his exemplum from *The Merchant of Venice* and quotes it in the introduction:

> The quality of mercy . . .
> is twice bless'd;
> It blesseth him that gives, and him that takes;
> 'Tis mightiest in the mightiest: it becomes
> The throned monarch better than his crown.

The text is kept constantly before the reader up to the closing words of the tale:

> "What dost thou know of suffering and oppression? I and my people know, but not thou."
> The reign of Edward VI was a singularly merciful one for those harsh times. Now that we are taking leave of him let us try to keep this in our minds, to his credit.

The theme is based upon the assumption of moral progress and enlightenment since the time of Edward VI. It was a view of progress that he later abandoned, maintaining that man had made progress in materialities only. But in *The Prince and the Pauper* Twain asserts by way of a general epilogue that mankind had made some moral progress. The assertion, however, is only incidental to his favorable contrast of the United States to another country still led by a king. No book by Twain fails in some way to reflect his hatred of monarchy, even an enlightened monarchy, and *The Prince and the Pauper* is no exception. The statement reflects Twain's motive in developing his theme of mercy and also indicates the theme that was to receive a fuller treatment in *A Connecticut Yankee*:

> One hears about the "hideous Blue-Laws of Connecticut," and is accustomed to shudder piously when they are mentioned. . . There has never been a time—under the Blue-Laws or any other —when above FOURTEEN crimes were punishable by death in Connecticut. But in England, within the memory of men who are still hale in body and mind, TWO HUNDRED AND TWEN-TY-THREE crimes were punishable by death! These facts are worth knowing—and worth thinking about, too.

The book is an historical romance, "Tale for Young People of All Ages," as the subtitle proclaims, and not a bad one. Indeed, in its day it was a positive advance over the usual fare offered to a juvenile audience. Twain was essentially a realist, and even a romance, he believed, should be told with realistic details. He contrasts the world of the court with that of the common people and does not stay his hand from painting the filth, poverty, drunkenness, and brutality of the people laboring under cruel and unjust laws. Twain portrayed the conditions as faithfully as his limited knowledge, gained from reading a few sources, would permit.

But even if one accepts the fantastic exchange of identity between the prince and the pauper that begins the tale, the following events cannot be said to proceed realistically. The numerous adventures involving the prince in his picaresque wanderings are no more unusual in their own cultural and historical setting than Huck Finn's in another time and place, but there is a vast difference between the two in the elementary forms of their treatment. Verisimilar details are supplied, but Twain does not really seem to desire the reader to feel any sense of immediacy in the events. In *Huckleberry Finn*, the reader feels himself to be present as events unfold before him, but in *The Prince and the Pauper* Twain reminds the reader that the events after all took place long ago; this is a legend that he is narrating for an audience: "It may be that the wise and the learned believed it in the old days; it may be that only the unlearned and the simple loved it and credited it." The reader is frequently reminded that he should not even pretend to be present.

> Let us skip a number of years.
> London was fifteen hundred years old, and was a great town—for that day. . . .
> Let us privileged ones hurry to the great banqueting room and have a glance at matters there while Tom is being made ready for the imposing occasion. . . .
> And so we leave them. . . .
> Let us go backwards a few hours. . . .
> Let us change the tense for convenience. . . .

Twain repeatedly addresses the reader directly and reminds him that he is outside them. The method does not follow the principle of making the events "seem reality." The numerous footnotes citing authorities for the actuality of the events portrayed cannot make them "seem reality"; indeed, in attempting to convince the reader of their truth, they only remind him more that the tale is fiction and not a chronicle of actuality.

Twain does not demonstrate any historical sense on a significant level. He asserts, for example, the naive notion that the common man reacts universally and fundamentally the same. Tom Canty, so far as Twain understood, in another time and place was a Tom Sawyer whose romantic dreams came true, but he had no conception that the difference in circumstances could also account for the differences in their characters. The assumption that the only difference between the prince and the pauper was in their clothing is manifestly absurd. Even if their raiment is symbolic, the proposition is untenable, but Twain persists in working it out to an improbable solution.

The Prince and the Pauper certainly is not a realistic view of mankind, or boyhood, distilled in the pages of pseudohistory. It may be regarded as a kind of legend and as such embodies an ideal that mankind should serve; but inevitably, in the light of his nature, man must fall short of achieving. The story is then directed to the mythic, primitive, juvenile mind, and to this mind it speaks a message: mankind is fundamentally good, and the virtues of charity, mercy, and magnanimity are inherent in man's nature. It is the message of *Huckleberry Finn* in another range of material. The two books, which he often worked on simultaneously, afford a striking contrast: although the beliefs about the nature of mankind informing both books are similar, *Huckleberry Finn* is more convincing because the body of belief is associated with the folk from which it sprang, while in *The Prince and the Pauper* it is forced upon an alien culture.

It is not distortion of the truth to say that *A Connecticut Yankee* follows *The Prince and the Pauper* in order of inception. It is true that *Huckleberry Finn* was published between the two works, but it was begun before *The Prince and the Pauper*. Preceding *A Connecticut Yankee* there were several years during which Twain produced no major fiction, and when he began *A Connecticut Yankee*, it was to be his last book. Thereafter he was to have supported his family as a businessman rather than as a novelist. His business ventures did not succeed, and *A Connecticut Yankee* was not his last book; he was to depend upon his writing for the remainder of his life as his chief source of income.

For the moment, *A Connecticut Yankee* can be regarded as a sort of epilogue to Mark Twain's career as a novelist, since he thought it would be his last novel. In it he intended to make his final judgment in fiction upon mankind. That he did not say his final word he realized after the book was completed: "Well, my book is written—let it go. But if I were only to write it over again there wouldn't be so many things left out. They burn in me; and they keep multiplying and multiplying; but now they can't ever be said. And besides, they would require a library—and a pen warmed-up in hell." [3]

Twain does not invent the facts of his book, but creates a fictional objectification of historical fact. He indicates as much in his preface:

> The ungentle laws and customs touched upon in this tale are historical, and the episodes which are used to illustrate them are also historical. It is not pretended that these laws and customs existed in England in the sixth century; no, it is only pretended that inasmuch as they existed in the English and other civilizations of far later times, it is safe to consider that it is no libel upon the sixth century to suppose them to have been in practice in that day also. One is quite justified in inferring that whatever one of these laws or customs was lacking in that remote time, its place was competently filled by a worse one.

His naive assumption that laws are progressively more oppressive as one goes farther back in time is predicated upon an equally naive assumption that human progress is associated with material progress. Twain is grossly ignorant of the role archaic institutions once played in the history of mankind. The whole institution of chivalry, for example, he regards as no more than irrational and glittering trappings in the service of suppressing and exploiting the common man; there is no awareness of it as an ethical code of conduct acknowledging an obligation toward the weak and less fortunate.

But knowledge of history is not the limit of Twain's ignorance revealed in *A Connecticut Yankee*; it extends to politics, economics, and religion—all involving fundamental problems that are of major concern in the book. His simple explanation of the economic value of money has the aroma of a politician justifying his views to his constituency. In politics he evinces the ardor of a young revolutionary who wants a "new deal" dealt over the body of the old. In matters religious he preaches the blind prejudice of the freethinker who will admit no impediments to his newly won freedom. The Church was no more than an institution dedicated to fostering superstition while living off the proceeds of oppression. The primitive mind is color-blind; it sees no hue or tint, only black and white.

This same naïveté extends to other aspects of the plot. Hank Morgan, head superintendent at an arms factory in Connecticut, sustains a blow on the head. When he recovers consciousness he finds himself captive in King Arthur's England in the year 528. He saves his life and gains a reputation as a wizard by claiming responsibility for an eclipse of the sun. The king makes him his right hand man with the title of Boss, and the Boss sets about modernizing the kingdom by introducing nineteenth-century technology in such forms as gunpowder, electricity, and telephones, all the time having to counter the forces of ignorance and superstition led by Merlin the Magician. After numerous picaresque adventures, the Boss is finally defeated by Merlin in cooperation with the Church.

Mark Twain could not have been entirely aware of the implications of the story he constructed. As so often is true of his efforts, there is a wide gap between intention and achievement. After completing the book he apparently had altered his understanding of the Yankee. He described him to the illustrator of the book as "a perfect ignoramus; he is boss of a machine shop; he can build a locomotive or a Colt's revolver, he can put up and run a telegraph line, but he's an ignoramus, nevertheless." [4] Critics have pointed out that for an ignoramus, the Yankee exhibits a startlingly wide variety of accomplishments as an administrator, astronomer, statesman, and technician. They find this a blemish; the Boss has no realistic right to be so talented. But Twain is correct, more right perhaps than he knew. The Boss is an ignoramus. He demonstrates the fact in his views on economics, religion, and politics, his technical achievements notwithstanding. But Twain himself shows no awareness of the Yankee's full ignorance.

Yet the disturbing fact remains that Twain has the Yankee merit the popular title of the Boss. By it he obviously intended to liken the Yankee to a foreman in charge of a large number of workers; but by virtue of his position, in another time he might have been designated *Der Führer* or *Il Duce*. A vexing problem presents itself: was Twain aware that he had created a political dictatorship upon a technocratic foundation? If he was conscious of the fact, then clearly he intended to say that the people will rise up against such a form of government; if not, then the conclusion has no more meaning than plausibly to restore history to its normal course after the interlude of an instructive adventure.

The latter motive is dictated by the demands of realism and must be assumed to be the probable one for Twain. Nowhere else does he seem to realize that he had attempted to create a monolithic society; indeed, the tone of his conclusion suggests regret that the forces of ignorance and superstition were strong enough to over-balance those of reason and to destroy what reason had created.

It may well be that although this book is marred to some extent by burlesque, bad taste, and naive assumptions, it is at the same time a prophetic work. Not, of course, deliberately prophetic, but Twain's commitment to democratic concepts, and his support of them by making what he felt to be a contrast with antidemocratic institutions, have raised the book to the level of prophecy because of the inherent issue of democracy *versus* autocracy in any such comparison. Democracy cannot function without an enlightened populace, but technological advancement does not necessarily bring with it enlightenment. The book, therefore, may be read as a criticism of nineteenth-century scientific achievement as well as of medieval ignorance. Thus read, it must also be placed against a background of Utopian fiction to which it is closely related. In a sense it is an answer to such a work as Bellamy's immediately popular *Looking Backward* (1888); *A Connecticut Yankee* (1889) also looks backward, but ironically. Knighthood may be ridiculed by the spectacle of a knight riding about the country as a traveling salesman, but the reader must finally be struck by the fact that nineteenth-century commercial travelers and their advertising methods also suffer by the comparison.

There is no evidence outside the book itself to indicate that Twain was aware of these implications in his work; on the contrary, he believed he had merely made a contrast between two periods in history to the advantage of the later one. The book raises large questions and offers partial answers, but in dealing with them, Twain demonstrates that he is entirely out of his depth. If he had done no more than he professed to attempt, *A Connecticut Yankee* would deserve little serious consideration. But there is more, and what remains saves the book, for it is what we value in Twain—his prose and his sympathy for the dignity of the individual man. He was better equipped to handle these assets on native grounds, but wherever Twain chose to roam—even to sixth-century England—he carried with him in some measure these virtues.

The moment the Yankee begins speaking, the reader knows what was missing in *The Prince and the Pauper*. In the earlier work Twain's own prose was too much affected by his effort to write a language he had never heard spoken. Even if we grant that his version of Tudor speech is accurate, it is nonetheless stilted, and even Twain's own language, in connecting narrative and descriptive links, too often parades mincingly by the reader. But from the mouth of the Yankee, the narrator of his own tale, flows colloquial, supple speech in prose perfectly adapted to his purpose:

> I am an American. I was born and reared in Hartford, in the State of Connecticut—anyway, just over the river, in the country. So I am a Yankee of the Yankees—and practical; yes, and nearly barren of sentiment, I suppose—or poetry, in other words. My father was a blacksmith, my uncle was a horse doctor, and I was both, along at first. Then I went over to the great arms factory and learned my real trade; learned all there was to it; learned to make everything: guns, revolvers, cannon, boilers, engines, all sorts of labor-saving machinery. Why I could make anything a body wanted—anything in the world, it didn't make any difference what; and if there wasn't any quick new fangled way to make a thing, I could invent one—and do it as easy as rolling off a log. I became head superintendent; had a couple of thousand men under me.

With easy drawling cadences the narrator relaxes and begins to spin his extended yarn. Like his progenitors, the tellers of tall tales, he begins with verisimilar details, commonplace facts, before ultimately leaping from realism to fantasy, burlesque, irony, satire, humorous digression, and common sense.

The Yankee maintains the character he delineates for himself for a time, but the pressure of the romantic circumstances in which he is involved proves too much for him. As the Boss he too often turns out to be a grown-up Tom Sawyer; instead of "practical; yes, and nearly barren of sentiment," he often becomes a day-dreamer manufacturing adventure.

> Well, I had gone and spoiled it again, made another mistake. A double one, in fact. There were plenty of ways to get rid of that officer by some simple and plausible device, but no, I must pick out a picturesque one; it is the crying defect of my character.

As a character, the Boss may not be entirely consistent or convincing, but he does display moments of greatness and magnanimity in his large sympathy for the weakness of others, and a certain sense of the dignity and rights of the individual man. He speaks then not as a practical Yankee or romantic Tom Sawyer, but as a warm-hearted, clear-sighted Huck Finn. In the smallpox hut he sees Arthur not as a king, but as a fellow man touched by the consequences of injustice and the degradation of a human being at the hands of another. With Sandy he is tolerant, gentle, and understanding. He makes one of the bitterest satiric commentaries upon aristocracy through Sandy: "When I saw her fling herself upon those hogs, with tears of joy running down her cheeks, and strain them to her heart, and kiss them, and caress them, and call them reverently by grand princely names, I was ashamed of her, ashamed of the human race." But he cannot in his heart condemn Sandy. Like Huck, when he confronts a situation that he cannot control, he accepts it. "It would be a waste of time to try to argue her out of her delusion, it couldn't be done; I must just humor it." And in the end Sandy becomes his adored wife, a source of amusement in her simplicity and the fount of all virtue in her womanhood. She is a thinly disguised Olivia, the object of Twain's earthly worship. And Clarence is as a son to the Boss, the product of his creation, who remains loyal and faithful to the end.

These characters remain true to Twain's underlying vision of man's moral responsibility and ultimately refute his pessimistic views of mankind's moral irresponsibility. He sets out to demonstrate mankind's moral depravity en masse and ends by asserting a person's fundamental bias toward moral right when he functions as a real human being. The two conclusions cannot rationally be reached from the same evidence. There is bound to be a resulting tension between the points of view. One is the consequence of assumptions implicit in Twain's style; the other is the product of attitudes imposed upon that style. Even while Twain was developing his jaundiced social views and venting his spleen upon certain institutions, he was creating characters not at all in accord with these opinions.

VII

The Road to
What Is Man?

WITHIN *A Connecticut Yankee* there was a divided viewpoint
toward the nature of mankind that tended to destroy coherence in
the work. The final attitude impressed upon the reader, however,
is that the author ultimately regards man as capable of dignity and
worth when he conducts himself as a morally responsible being.
Indeed, man's moral nature is the chief difference between him
and the brutes. Twain ironically expressed the fact in one of
Pudd'nhead Wilson's maxims: "If you pick up a starving dog and
make him prosperous, he will not bite you. This is the principal
difference between a dog and a man." [1] Twain's sympathy, even
to the end, was always drawn to this moral view of mankind, but
his rational development was increasingly in an opposite direction.

During the period following publication of *A Connecticut
Yankee,* he began to codify his pessimistic rational views in his
private "bible," which eventually appeared as *What Is Man?* All
of his later work is dominated by the mechanistic ideas expressed
there. This mechanistic concept denied that man was a morally
responsible creature and thus robbed Twain's work of its chief
vitalizing force. His creative work after 1888 is a chronicle of
shifts and dodges to avoid the logical consequence of his developed rational position; his feeling would not allow him to express
the inevitable conclusion to his pessimism—that there is no meaning in a life robbed of moral responsibility. Such a life is not
worth the living, and many times Twain expressed this conclusion in disconnected statements outside his fiction. Perhaps a

glimpse of this result informed his comment that "Of the demonstrably wise there are but two; those who commit suicide and those who keep their reasoning faculties atrophied with drink." [2] Twain's pessimism logically coincides with his mechanistic philosophy.

It is obvious to anyone who reads all of Twain's novels that some of them, in their inception and in their development of incidents, depart from his best and most characteristic achievement. In each such instance the "philosopher" works at variance with the novelist. Twain could not see the logical relation between the technique of realism and a body of philosophical principles. So far as he was concerned, realism was only the method by which any subject could be rendered believable and "seem reality."

Consequently, when Twain thinks like a novelist (that is, when, by means of his own simple, humorous, honest style, he as novelist concerns himself with the creation of simple, honest, humorous creatures and their affairs), he is capable of achieving a coherent statement with which he was qualified to deal. But when he tries to think like a philosopher and impose a preconceived pattern of behavior illustrating some ideological concept upon his material, the result is less than satisfactory as a novel. One is forced to criticize him on his own terms and to find many of his novels inadequate in the quality of his ideas, more than in the manner of their statement.

Fortunately for his art, however, Twain did not see clearly the implications of his conscious position, for he continued throughout his life to concern himself with the affairs of a worthless human race. And in spite of, even in opposition to, his bitter pessimism, he continued to achieve, even in his late work, some measure of spasmodic control over his art; but never could he equal his peak achievement, which was not dominated by his later ideas of determinism.

His work of permanent value reflects a different conception of reality, one based upon a scheme of more universally accepted truths regarding the nature of man and his relation to God and his fellows. As a legacy of his frontier development, Twain unwittingly accepted a body of folk belief of an essentially primitive cast of mind, a body of assumptions universal among all folk peoples in all ages. The basic assumption from which all primitive symptoms derive is that the folk mind is richer and fuller than any savant's brain. The assumption is at the base of all of the westerner's reactions of implicit superiority when confronted with the civilizations of the eastern states or Europe. The humor in *The Innocents Abroad* is founded upon this assumption of folk superiority. The elemental mind is somehow superior to the more complex but morally corrupt civilized mind; thus the child and childlike points of view gain ideological stature in the folk mind.

The relation of these attitudes to romanticism is readily apparent, and undoubtedly these are the elements which have led some critics to a concern with Twain's paradoxical romantic versus antiromantic conflict. These primitive notions are a part of Twain's early belief; as he developed in his thinking, he tried to supplant them with his growing deterministic ideas. Since they were an inherent part of his feelings and belief, however, they continued to inform his work even while he was consciously formulating contrary ideas and seeking to apply them in his writing.

Twain was not a clear thinker, and in this fact lay his artistic salvation. His avowed beliefs, such as those expounded in *What Is Man?*, and the ideas implicit in his best work often have little in common, even at times contradict one another. The determinism incipient in his early work is fragmentary and does only occasional damage. Most of that work, however inept it seems at times, is solidly founded upon moral issues involved in the human struggle. It is only relatively late that he pushes his ideas into any semblance of coherence, and they then spell out a rigid deterministic theory that allows man no freedom of choice to alter his mode of existence. Twain's theory denies the possibility of conflict or struggle in human affairs; they are only illusions, and literature is robbed of its chief animating experience. He contends that men are mere robots incapable of moral struggle. We find in the course of his work an increasing conflict between a craft founded on the assumption of free will and his late insistence upon his deterministic doctrines. The conflict destroys coherent statement.

It is not surprising that Twain should rebel against the God of his childhood. The temper of the times made such a course inevitable for anyone who resented tyranny. The impact of modern science upon traditional concepts was then beginning to be felt in the popular mind, and scientific achievement had no more devoted admirer than Twain. It was the beginning of the present age of the decay of faith. Its chief symptom and consequence is pessimism, and Twain was the first pessimist in modern American literature. In January, 1905, he made the following entry in his notebook: "Sixty years ago optimist and fool were not synonymous terms. This is a greater change than that wrought by science and invention. It is the mightiest change that was ever wrought in the world in any sixty years since creation." [3]

Both his formal religious training and his questioning of its validity were probably fostered by his parents. His mother was a Presbyterian and required him to go to Sunday School and church, where he heard the Calvinistic doctrines of hell-fire, predestination, and God's wrath preached every week. In addition, his mother and older sister Pamela saw to it that he, like Huck Finn, regularly read the Bible as the literal word of God. But his father was said to have been a freethinker, and young Sam Clemens must certainly have heard these doctrines questioned. This training, of course, had its effect. The Christian religion for him thereafter was always represented by the stern strictures of Calvinism, and he was never able to conceive of God as other than anthropomorphic until the formulation of his "bible."

A certain Scotsman named MacFarlane, with whom Twain associated in Cincinnati when he was twenty-one, is supposed to have completed Twain's emancipation from the strict theology of his mother's church; but even if the story was true, it was only an apparent emancipation. In fact, Twain was never entirely emotionally freed from the grip of Calvinism. For a long time he struggled between doubt and fear. In a distressed and sentimental letter written shortly after the death of his brother Henry in 1858 he said, "I,—even I,—have humbled myself to the ground and prayed as never man prayed before." [4] And after a period of time in the far West spent in what Olivia could regard as no more than a life of sin, he apparently made a sincere effort to reform and embrace more orthodox views about God and the good life. Certainly his letters to his wife reflect his reading of the Bible, church attendance, prayers, and his trust in God—all doubtless calculated to please Livy. A. B. Paine, his biographer, records that prayers and Bible reading were part of the household routine of his early marriage, but the custom seems soon to have fallen into disuse.[5]

During the Buffalo period he wrote,

> To trust the God of the Bible is to trust an irascible, vindictive, fierce and ever fickle and changeful master; to trust the true God is to trust a Being who has uttered no promises, but whose beneficent, exact, and changeless ordering of the machinery of his colossal universe is proof that he is at least steadfast to his purpose; whose unwritten laws, so far as they affect man, being equal and impartial, show that he is just and fair; these things taken together, suggest that if he shall ordain us to live hereafter, he will still be steadfast, just, and fair toward us. We shall not need to require anything more.[6]

He rejects the God of the Old Testament, but, more significantly, he affirms a God who is not so grim, one who is if anything kindly disposed toward a mechanism which he has set in motion, good eighteenth-century Deistic doctrine.

When Twain moved his family to Hartford in late 1871, he joined the community of Nook Farm and there moved in a society that genteelly followed the faith of a liberal Congregationalism. Most of his neighbors had rejected the Calvinism of their early youth and had embraced the lukewarm romanticism left as a legacy by Horace Bushnell; in short, they turned religion over to the personal mystical experience of the individual, leaving the way open for one to believe almost anything. Twain nominally became a member of Joseph Twichell's church, but this move was apparently dictated by motives of social expediency and personal friendship rather than any sincere conviction. It did, however, provide a climate permitting him to hold his own views. He still persisted in his rejection of a stern God conceived by Calvin, as did the other members of the Nook Farm community.

Here his apostasy ends. Requiring nothing more of God, he turns his contemplation back toward the world as a more fruitful field for investigation, and it is with the moral world that he is largely concerned. This conception of God and moral law he later defined more fully. Paine places the following statement in the early 1880's, generally during the period in which he wrote *Huckleberry Finn*. Apparently it was not intended for publication but was set down for his own guide as a testament, possibly one of many jottings out of which grew his philosophy contained in *What Is Man?*:

> I believe in God the almighty.
> I do not believe he has ever sent a message to a man by anybody. . . .
> I think the goodness, the justice and the mercy of God are manifested in his works: I perceive that they are manifested toward me in this life; the logical conclusion is that they will be manifested toward me in the life to come, if there should be one.
> I do not believe in special providences. I believe that the universe is governed by strict and immutable laws. . . .
> I believe that the world's moral laws are the outcome of the world's experience. It needed no God to come down out of heaven to tell men that murder and theft and the other immoralities were bad, both for the individual who commits them and for society which suffers from them.
> If I break all these moral laws I cannot see how I injure God by it, for He is beyond the reach of injury from me—I could as easily injure a planet by throwing mud at it. It seems to me that my misconduct could only injure me and other men. I cannot benefit God by obeying these moral laws—I could as easily benefit the planet by withholding my mud. (Let these sentences be read in the light of the fact that I believe I have moral laws only from man—none whatever from God.) Consequently I do not see why I should be either punished or rewarded hereafter for the deeds I do here.[7]

Despite the attributes of goodness, justice, and mercy which Twain assigns to God, his total conception seems to emphasize the impersonal character of such a deity. There is no bond between the individual and his creator. Man cannot call upon any force outside his world. Such a decline of faith, of course, intensifies the claim of the actual. The individual is driven to a greater absorption in immediate realities that he can get a firm hold on.

This conception of God was little altered during the remainder of Twain's life; it was the key doctrine in his creed. Though the major outlines of this view did not change, Twain did modify his attitude and shifted his emphasis of certain points. In 1898 he wrote, "God's inhumanity to man makes countless thousands mourn." [8] It is characteristic of his later opinion that if God does have any attitude toward mankind, it is a malignant instead of a benign interest. But such a shift in Twain's tone attends his increasingly pessimistic view of the human race rather than results from direct speculation upon the nature of God, for his interest continued to the end, as it always had focused upon the moral character of mankind.

God's creatures more than God himself interest Mark Twain, and his lifelong interest ended with his defining man's position in the "damned human race." There is more to the expletive than a mild oath; Twain chose his words carefully, and by damned he meant that the race of man deserved condemnation.

But he did not always believe this. He was also capable of believing in the idea of progress. Such apparent contradictions and paradoxes in Twain's thinking exist because he found it difficult to make final decisions on fundamental issues. The progress of his mental growth is not a logical movement from idea to idea, from one position to a succeeding one founded on the previous. Instead, his mental faculties are concerned with constructing rational defenses for positions arrived at by emotional paths.

Twain once said, "We all do no end of feeling, and we mistake it for thinking." [9] It is, of course, the way of the artist rather than the philosopher, and one treads dangerously close to the borders of sanity when he proceeds irrationally under the delusion that his behavior is perfectly rational. What could Twain make of the fact that he could condemn the entire human race and in the next breath praise certain members? With such a lack of disciplined control over his rational faculties, Twain inspires one to wonder not at his pessimism but at his ability to continue any sort of meaningful literary activity at all. "When we remember that we are all made in God's image, the mysteries disappear and life stands explained." [10] Persistence in such views can lead only to despair.

Twain regards the vast panorama of human activity in its many forms. At first he is moved to comment upon man's foibles from the point of view of the humorist. He makes of man's error a subject for laughter and consequent ridicule. In this course the humorist as a moralist is optimistic in that he implies a corrective and the belief in the possibility of human improvement. But through his representation of truth as he sees it, he comes to a recognition of an inexplicably harsh destiny awaiting every man born into the world. This view is implicit in all tragedy. Twain never read Sophocles, but often he echoes the tragedian's view that next to not being born at all the greatest prize that man can win is an early death. It is ironic that the greatest humorist America produced came to a final recognition of the inescapable tragic fact of human existence. His ordeal was that he was ill-equipped to cope with this recognition. As a humorist he had developed a realistic technique adequate for his purpose. Such a technique applied to essentially tragic matter produced cynicism. Humor inhibits any tragic resolution; it is antithetical to a spirit of reverent acceptance of man's tragic fate.

The books after *Huckleberry Finn* to a greater or less degree pull in opposite directions between a comic rendering of events and an essentially tragic feeling for their high seriousness. Caught in a dilemma, characteristically he cannot choose; he attempts the impossible of holding both attitudes at once and formulates his credo of cynical pessimism which reduces man to a mere automaton. For a professed realist, an antiromanticist, it is curious that he comes full circle back to the basic position of the romantic, that automatism is desirable in the self-expressing man. The determinist believes that man inevitably is motivated only by outside influences, whereas the romantic believes that man should submit himself to be motivated only by divine influence manifesting itself within. But, of course, Yvor Winters has observed that determinism is romanticism in a disillusioned mood.[11]

Mark Twain's moralism was the outgrowth of intense sympathy for his fellow man; his determinism developed from antipathy. Never a disciplined thinker, he drifted rather than developed from a mostly sympathetic to a mostly antipathetic attitude. So long as he was a promising literary figure on his way to success, ambition forced him to exercise some measure of control over his feelings; but once he had arrived and become a privileged figure, he could let himself go and give vent to his varying moods of temper and rage. The sad truth, undoubtedly oversimplified, is that Twain's increasing lack of control over his art is a reflection of his own increasing lack of self-control. In 1909 he wrote,

> I have been punished many and many a time, and bitterly, for doing things and reflecting afterward, but these tortures have been of no value to me; I still do the thing commanded by Circumstance and Temperament, and reflect afterward. Always violently. When I am reflecting on these occasions, even deaf persons can hear me think.[12]

In spite of many efforts to demonstrate early foreshadowing of Twain's pessimism, the fact seems to remain that it developed relatively late. Undoubtedly personal misfortunes played a part. The loss of his fortune, Suzy's sudden death, the loss of his wife, and finally Jean's death—all these events took their toll in anxiety and sorrow and contributed to Twain's increasing bitterness.

Pessimism is incongruous in a youth, and Twain retained his youth a long time. As he pointed out, "There is no sadder sight than a young pessimist, except an old optimist." [13] Actually, there is little to suggest that Twain was any different from other young men in his optimism regarding his own future. When he was eighteen and away from home for the first time, he wrote from Philadelphia to his brother, Orion, "Downhearted, the devil! I have not had a particle of such a feeling since I left Hannibal, more than four months ago." [14] He was optimistic enough about the world in general to believe in its capabilities of betterment.

Years later he wrote to Frank E. Burrough, with whom he roomed for a time when a young man, "You have described a callow fool, a self-sufficient ass, a mere tumble-bug, stern in air, heaving at his bit of dung, imagining that he is remodeling the world and is entirely capable of doing it right. . . . That is what I was at 19-20." [15] This statement, of course, reflects the jaundiced opinion of a much older Twain. But the young man was a reformer, and so long as he was committed to a vision of man's possibilities of betterment, he cannot be said to have been a pessimist.

Twain's pessimism repeatedly seems to arise in almost every area of inquiry concerning the man and his work. We have already observed that the feelings which impelled him to fashion his deterministic bible were pessimistic ones. If by pessimism we mean an attitude that regards life as essentially evil and the whole scheme of existence wrong or bad, that believes in the preponderance of unhappiness over happiness in life, then certainly Twain was a pessimist. We have already observed, for example, how he later came to regard the universe as evil because it was at the mercy of an indifferent, if not actually malignant, spirit.

Twain himself said, "The man who is a pessimist before 40 knows too much; if he is an optimist after it, he knows too little." [16] Near his seventieth birthday he wrote, "Pessimists are born not made; optimists are born not made; but no man is born either pessimist wholly or optimist wholly, perhaps; he is pessimistic along certain lines and optimistic along certain others. That is my case." [17] The problem of understanding Twain's pessimism becomes one of discovering along which lines he was pessimistic and which optimistic.

We discover, of course, that there are no clearcut distinctions. Twain is capable of both pessimistic and optimistic judgments about the same subject. He is most pessimistic about the "damned human race." And the source of his attitude is not, as some critics would have us believe, that he felt man incapable of perfecting himself. His rage is directed at the fact that man falls so far short of his capabilities. In numerous instances he commented upon the progress man has made in humanitarian directions. But he sees no cause for rejoicing, for there remains much room for improvement, and the rate of improvement is slow. Twain impatiently fumes at the time required: " 'From age to age'—yes, it describes that giddy gait." [18] It is the pessimism of an idealist who realizes the remoteness of his ideal, but despite the bitterness of his views, Twain remained to the end a compassionate man and an admirer of honesty, justice, and kindness in others.

The impulse to reform long remained a dominant trait in Twain's make-up. Indeed, as late as 1901 a newspaper article referred to him in these terms: "The genial humorist of the earlier day is now a reformer of the vigorous kind, a sort of knight errant who does not hesitate to break a lance with either Church or State." [19] The unknown writer, of course, misjudged the change which had taken place. Twain had always been a reformer, but the satire had been leavened by humor.

In his later years Twain's verbal criticisms were widely quoted in the public press, generally without any humorous context, and they were hardly views motivated by the desire to reform, but rather caustic observations on the "damned human race" and its insane conduct.

The sketches and burlesques of his journalistic days usually had some satiric purpose. The earliest, dating from his Hannibal apprenticeship, were personal satire, more often trivial than serious. In Nevada and California he broadened his range of criticism and became a social satirist. But he still often indulged in personal satire as well, and the targets of his wrath were as likely to be superficial as important. In the main, however, he was emotionally on the side of right and justice in his criticisms of juries, legislatures, public officials, corporations, oppression, and pretension, although intellectually he could still approve of such institutions as a "paternal imperialism," which protected native areas while it introduced questionable social advantages. Often his humorous techniques ran out of control in the direction of a mere joke at the expense of satiric effect.

In later years he was able to see social injustices more profoundly. He was not, for example, taken in by pious claims of rescuing the Filipinos and extending the benefits of Americanism; he saw the Spanish-American War for what it was, an imperialistic grab. But by this time (1905), he saw little hope for social progress keeping up with material progress.

> Well, the 19th century made progress—the first progress after "ages and ages"—colossal progress. In what? Materialities. Prodigious acquisitions were made in things which add to the comfort of many and make life harder for as many more. But the addition to righteousness? Is that discoverable? I think not. The materialities were not invented in the interests of righteousness. . . .
> Did England rise against the infamy of the Boer War? No—rose in favor of it. Did America rise against the infamy of the Phillipine [sic] war? No—rose in favor of it. . . . Has the kingdom of God advanced in Russia since the beginning of time?
> Or in Europe and America, considering the vast backward step

of the money-lust? Or anywhere else? If there has been any progress toward righteousness since the early days of Creation—which, in my ineradicable honesty, I am obliged to doubt—I think we must confine it to ten percent of the population of Christendom.[20]

His humorous pronouncements are cynically pessimistic rather than satiric. "The universal brotherhood of man is our most precious possession—what there is of it." [21] Rationally he finds that man is no more than a machine, "a mere coffee-mill . . . his sole and piteously humble function being to grind coarse or fine, according to his make, outside impulses doing all the rest." [22] But at the same time Twain could never quite overcome his feeling of affection for his fellow man. "God puts something good and something lovable in every man His hands create." [23] And an entry in his notebook in 1890 observes, "That government is not best which best secures mere life and property—there is a more valuable thing—manhood." [24]

The story of Twain as a moralist is a bit different, for he did not substantially change his views on morality from the time he first established his fame as a moralist until his death nearly half a century later. He regarded moral law as the outcome of the world's experience. "I have received moral laws *only* from man—none whatever from God." [25] Furthermore, he believed that moral standards are relative; they are undergoing constant change.[26] The most common observation Twain makes about moral standards, however, concerns the often wide gap between morals professed and those practiced. "It has always been a peculiarity of the human race that it keeps two sets of morals in stock—the private and real, and the public and artificial." [27] "There are two kinds of Christian morals, one private and the other public. These two are so distinct, so unrelated, that they are no more akin to each other than are archangels and politicians." [28] This theme enters in varying degrees into almost all of Twain's fiction.

Despite the impression Twain sometimes gives that he would discard moral law, just as Huck and Tom shuck their confining clothes, the fact is that he believed moral law to be necessary. "A man should not be without morals; it is better to have bad morals than none at all." [29] He pointed out that man is the servant of convention: ". . . we could not subsist, either in a savage or a civilized state, without conventions; . . . we must accept them and stand by them, even when we disapproved [*sic*] of them." [30] His only basis for judging moral law was a pragmatic question: does the moral principle in practice achieve good or bad results? "The most permanent lessons in morals are those which come, not of booky teachings but of experience." [31]

Twain's efforts as a moralist are directed toward making life more endurable. He can approve of material progress in that it makes the lot of man easier. But, since man lives not by bread alone, he can at the same time condemn the lack of progress in righteousness. This view of the moralist-reformer as one who would make the world a better (i.e., more tolerable) place is opposed to the pessimist, not so much because the moralist is an idealist and consequently in some measure an optimist, but rather because the moralist is motivated by a compassion for his fellow man, who he simultaneously asserts is worthless. We may note the inconsistency, but it is more to the point to observe that Twain's most valuable and lasting work is informed by a large compassion and sympathy for the weakness of man.

It is curious that Twain seems unaware of this conflict between his compassionate feelings and his bitter philosophy. The conflict is not merely between feeling and emotion on one hand and intellect on the other. Twain's feelings were founded upon ideas embodied in the primitive folk mind, and therefore the conflict may be viewed also as one between two different modes of recognition. The conflict existed not because it could not be resolved but because Twain was unaware of it.

The conflict is not significantly present in his best early books —that is to say, in *Tom Sawyer* or *Huckleberry Finn*. Its earliest appearance was in *The Prince and the Pauper*. In that work the prince was made to go through a series of adventures which enlightened him as to the indignities heaped upon his subjects by unjust laws. Environmental circumstances modified his character and tempered his subsequent short reign with a justice unusual for those times. Meanwhile Twain recounts the progress of Tom Canty, the bogus prince, from a righteous indignation at social injustice to a gradual resignation and acceptance of his position.

His corruption is completed by the time he denounces his mother. To this point, Twain's view of circumstances molding the prince and the beggar is consistent, but then he "flies the logic track," to employ his own phrase. Tom's moral conscience takes over, and the deterministic thesis of the book falls apart.

> The words "I do not know you, woman!" were falling from Tom Canty's lips when this piteous thing occurred; but it smote him to the heart to see her treated so; . . . she seemed so wounded, so broken-hearted, that a shame fell upon him which consumed his pride to ashes, and withered his stolen royalty. His grandeurs were stricken valueless; they seemed to fall away from him like rotten rags. . . . He neither saw nor heard. Royalty had lost its grace and sweetness; its pomps were become a reproach. Remorse was eating his heart out. He said, "Would God I were free of my captivity!"
> He had unconsciously dropped back into the phraseology of the first days of his compulsory greatness.

One other example of the conflict will suffice; it is to be found in "The Man That Corrupted Hadleyburg." In this story Twain sets up almost laboratory conditions for the working out of his mechanistic tale. The stranger motivates the deterministic action by contriving circumstances which will entrap the citizens of Hadleyburg. He knows they have no wills of their own, no inner resources to protect them from the consequences of their greed. And to a man the citizens fall into the trap, thus illustrating their inability to exercise any independent moral control.

So convincingly is the story contrived that the reader rarely observes that the determinism is not consistently applied. The derision of the courtroom audience holds each of the leading citizens morally responsible for his behavior; indeed, the two old people gain the reader's sympathy by holding themselves morally responsible, and they die of broken hearts, grief-stricken at their own perfidy. This last story was the best compromise Twain was to make between his sympathies and his deterministic philosophy, but even here the synthesis is not adequately effected.

In each of the instances cited, Twain was unable consistently to maintain his deterministic point of view. Lacking knowledge of the foundation in belief for his realistic style, he could not prevent his sympathetic feelings from upsetting his deterministic scheme of delineating character or incident inconsistent with his conscious views. Tom Canty redeems himself illogically in the face of the mechanistic deterioration of his character; the Boss is a machine set in motion only by hereditary factors, but illogically cherishes his inner moral force; and the moral character of the citizens of Hadleyburg was dictated by outward circumstances over which they had no control, but, nonetheless, illogically they are also held responsible for their moral behavior.

VIII
Symbols of Despair

BERNARD DEVOTO employed the term "symbols of despair" in referring to the "bewildered groping" quality of Twain's writing growing out of the nineties. Most of this writing was unpublished, and in DeVoto's words "the abandoned efforts make an astonishing, a heartbreaking bulk, perhaps fifteen thousand pages." What concerned DeVoto was the quality of despair that grew out of the series of personal tragedies and misfortunes in Twain's life. They were reflected in his writing, in the fumbling and often confused attempts to answer questions he could hardly even frame. *What Is Man?* and *The Mysterious Stranger* were two of the fruits of this attempt.

DeVoto discusses the great bulk of unpublished manuscripts as symbols of the disordered and groping state of Twain's mind under the shock of misfortune. But it would seem that this is only the buried, private part of a struggle that Twain was carrying on publicly and symbolically in most of his work published after *A Connecticut Yankee*. In many of these published pieces, Twain was consciously using symbols to extend the realistic craft he had mastered earlier. The unhappy fact is that he was ill-equipped to do so. Not until *The Mysterious Stranger* and "The Man That Corrupted Hadleyburg" did he achieve some degree of control over the symbolic method that he was slowly evolving during these years.

Twain's work after *A Connecticut Yankee* accelerates in its turn from the objective rendering of intimate personal experience founded upon assumptions of some universality to regarding his experience as evidence supporting a philosophy of limited appeal and demonstrable fallacy. His humor gradually degenerates to caustic barbs of cynical pessimism. His philosophy in robbing human character of moral responsibility also robs a fictional character of interest, since its chief claim to our attention rests upon its confronting moral dilemmas. The wonder is that Twain's later work still commands an audience at all, and the reason is that some of it is still held above mediocrity by the strength of his craft. His later work is rewarding to the student, if not the general reader, as examples of the writer's struggle to continue his art, trying to refute his rational view that the attempt is futile.

The American Claimant followed three years after *A Connecticut Yankee*. It fails from almost every point of view and represents the nadir of Twain's career as a writer of fiction, but it does deserve some mention for its relation to *A Connecticut Yankee*, for in a way it is a commentary upon the issues raised in that book. *The American Claimant* was a rehash of a play he had written in collaboration with Howells, but the play itself had been a warmed-over version of material suggested by the dramatization of *The Gilded Age*. The end product was a literary stew with few bits of nourishing meat.

The only son and heir to the Earl of Rossmore decides to renounce his inheritance in favor of an American claimant, Colonel Mulberry Sellers. He travels to America with his head full of the democratic notions he associates with the American dream, and there he decides to make his way disguised as a penniless Englishman in search of work. A series of misadventures befalls him that has the effect of revealing his ideals as illusions. Eventually he meets Colonel Sellers and falls in love with his daughter.

Surrounded by the nonsense and tomfoolery concerning Sellers —no real relation to the Sellers of *The Gilded Age*—there are a few telling points concerning America. It is the same America that Twain contrasted with the Middle Ages in *A Connecticut Yankee*, but in *The American Claimant* it receives an ironic examination. The theme concerns the problem of appearance and reality—the wide disparity between the principles that appear to operate in American society and those which actually do operate. The ironic theme is not subtle; it should not have been missed by such a critic as Van Wyck Brooks, who writes of Twain that he "had fully accepted the illusion of his contemporaries that the progress of machinery was identical with the progress of humanity." [1] There is perhaps some excuse for missing the irony of the clerk's eulogy upon opportunity in America during the Mechanics' Club debate. The excuse would be that one did not go on to read the beginning of the following chapter:

> During the first few days he [the young Englishman] kept the fact diligently before his mind that he was in a land where there was "work and bread for all." In fact, for convenience's sake he fitted it to a little tune and hummed it to himself; but as time wore on the fact itself began to take on a doubtful look, and next the tune got fatigued and presently ran down and stopped.

There is no need to go on listing other evidence that Twain wanted the reader to see the irony involved in his comparison between democratic ideals and actualities in America. The signs are clearly posted along the way.

Because Twain limited his theme to illustrating the conflict between aristocratic behavior and democratic ideals in America, his ideas are sounder than they appeared in *A Connecticut Yankee*. The visiting nobleman can record an observation in his diary: "It does rather look as if in a republic where all are free and equal prosperity and position constitute rank." And the pronouncement rings true because it is not founded upon any dubious assumptions about history, politics, or religion, but rather reflects direct observation of firsthand experience. Twain is dealing with a life and time that he knew intimately. The ideas not only complement those of *A Connecticut Yankee*, but also supplement those in *The Gilded Age*.

The American Claimant, however much it may interest the student of Twain, is a bad novel. Undoubtedly Twain wished to capitalize upon the success of Colonel Sellers as a character in *The Gilded Age* and the play based upon the book. But the fool who passes for Colonel Sellers in *The American Claimant* is a travesty upon the original character. Mental incompetence is offensive as a subject of humor, and this Colonel Sellers is a madman. Moreover, cheap theatrical claptrap constantly gets in the way of Twain's fundamentally serious theme. And finally, not one character is more than a wooden caricature. The book is unique among all of Twain's novels in that it does not offer even one redeeming, believable character to reward the reader, and it thus lacks the one essential of Twain's genius. Although it concerns a basically worthy subject, the novel does not in any way reflect the craft of which Twain was capable and attained even on occasions when he was dealing with material unworthy of his skill.

When Mark Twain hastily penned *The American Claimant*, it was clear to him that *A Connecticut Yankee* was not to be his last book. His business ventures had gone awry, and he had to continue to support his family by his pen. Hope for and belief in the Paige typesetting machine had not yet been lost, but until it could bring Twain a fortune he needed money, and the only way he could make it was by his writing. Under economic pressure Twain presents a painful spectacle in his attempts to recapture his former commercial successes. *The American Claimant* was ready at hand in dramatic form and was probably the easiest and quickest asset he could convert into cash. Soon after a false attempt at manufacturing another travel book in *Down The Rhone*, he tried to exploit the earlier success of his Hannibal material. Out of many starts he managed to finish *Tom Sawyer Abroad*, *Pudd'nhead Wilson*, and *Tom Sawyer Detective* in the order named. In addition, during these three years from 1891 to 1895, he also wrote *Joan of Arc*, a number of tales and sketches, and most of his critical essays as well as a mass of material never published.

The fiction does not reach the achievement of his earlier work; it would appear that he produced a great quantity at the expense of quality. But there are spasmodic moments during this period when some of Twain's magic returned to him for a time. And even in their mediocrity these works are valuable for affording some insight into Twain's greatness. Little of the early Twain, however, is displayed in *Tom Sawyer Detective*. The interest of this short novel centers almost entirely in the incredible plot. Twain's assurance by way of a footnote that the events were real reveals the limit of his conception of realism:

> Strange as the incidents of this story are, they are not inventions, but facts—even to the public confession of the accused. I

take them from an old-time Swedish criminal trial, change the actors, and transfer the scenes to America.

The events, however, have little to do with the characters; there is no integration of the two. Huck tells the story, but he is not the Huck from the earlier saga on the river. He is no more than an illiterate Dr. Watson to Tom's smart-alecky Sherlock Holmes. The two characters have fallen in status from the level of great literature down to the role of stock characters in a juvenile series such as Tom Swift or The Rover Boys.

Stripped of all the "thrill and stir and seeming of reality," bereft of all the elements animating the pages of Twain's best achievement, *Tom Sawyer Detective* emerges as no more than the skeleton of a novel bearing a faint resemblance to Twain's earlier work. What is left is only a small version in tired prose of the same story he had so well told before. It is still the story of a boy who becomes a hero, but the heroics are cheap and theatrical.

Tom Sawyer Abroad at first glance would appear to be of the same order. The airship obtrudes and wings the trio of innocents —Tom, Huck, and Jim—off into a fantastic adventure. Actually the worst blemish is the usual one for Twain in his later period of writing: the story lacks polish; it comes to a grinding halt rather than an appropriate conclusion, as if the author's imagination had quit on him. At an earlier date he would have revised the work and invented incidents to pad it out to full novel length.

The essential story is all present. The boy's dream of becoming a hero comes true, but this frame is only the vehicle for the profounder story that unfolds. The airship carries Tom, Huck, and Jim into space, where they can look down upon this globe of earth and upon the ant-men scurrying about its face. The three innocents are situated like Philip Traum in *The Mysterious Stranger*, but their superior relation to the earth is quite different. They are very much a part of the planet while still observing it from their exalted position. The three can take a detached view of man while themselves behaving quite humanly. From their distant view there is little discoverable difference between man and beast: "It was strange and unnatural to see lion eat lion." Their detachment explains the inferiority of the book to *Huckleberry*

Finn; Tom Sawyer Abroad lacks the sense of immediacy and power—of life being lived—that marks the earlier work. The loss is only partially compensated by the gain in symbolic value. But if it is a lesser achievement, it nonetheless has a share of the greatness of *Huckleberry Finn* in the nobility of the central characters.

The contrast between man en masse and the individuals in the balloon symbolizes Twain's dilemma during the latter part of his career—his inability to reconcile his emotional and intellectual attitudes toward a race that he felt deserved damnation, but whose individuals he often could not help loving. Seen from the balloon, man is no better than an animal, his behavior just as unmoral and irrational. Meanwhile, within the balloon there evolves among Jim, Huck, and Tom a drama that refutes the distant view of mankind on the ground.

The story that unfolds in the balloon is an exploration of the complexities of the primitive mind. Twain knew well how rich and complex that mind is, and how misleading is the sophisticated conception of the simple mind. Actually, the more self-conscious sophisticated mind is simpler in that it is relatively ordered, more under the control of rational forces attempting to impose some coherence. The primitive mind, on the other hand, is a complex and tangled jungle of half assimilated forces unaware of their inconsistencies. Such a mind has a much looser pattern of organization. It is simple only in the sense of being relatively unsubtle and, therefore, incapable of the distinctions possible for the more sophisticated intelligence. This difference does not deny the possibility of shrewdness and power of native intelligence to the primitive mind; it rather describes a difference in the mode of operation. One mind is the product of formal education; the other is the heritage of the folk. The two tend to be suspicious of one another when they lack a common meeting ground, for one is essentially aristocratic and the other elementally democratic.

Each of three characters in *Tom Sawyer Abroad* represents a slightly different aspect of the primitive mind. Jim functions on the level of superstition in all areas outside his own immediate, firsthand experience. Huck is similar except that he attempts to translate things strange to him into terms of his limited experience. Tom, unlike the other two, has read and misread books and thus acquired a veneer of sophistication. All have in common a folk heritage derived from their village, and all share a wide sympathy for their fellow man. Part of the time Tom assumes the role of the sophisticate; much of the fun comes from his discomfort at the minor triumphs scored by the primitive minds of Huck and Jim. But the veneer occasionally cracks, revealing Tom's essentially primitive rationale. A sophisticated mind, for example, will look up a strange word in a dictionary; not so the primitive. Huck was troubled by Tom's use of the word *welkin*:

> Tom explained the best he could. He said when a person made a big speech the newspapers said the shouts of the people made the welkin ring. He said they always said that, but none of them ever told what it was, so he allowed it just meant outdoors and up high. Well, that seemed sensible enough, so I was satisfied, and said so.

The common meeting ground of the three characters is their sympathy for their fellow man and their reverence for life. Suspicious of intellectual superiority, the three are nevertheless saddened by the death of the professor: ". . . we set there huddled up in the bow, and talked low about the poor professor; and everybody was sorry for him, and sorry the world had made fun of him and treated him so harsh. . . ." And Huck's ironic explanation of why he decided not to become an "ornithologer" is as fine as any passage in *Huckleberry Finn*:

> The minute Tom begun to talk about birds I judged he was a goner, because Jim knowed more about birds than both of us put together. You see, he had killed hundreds and hundreds of them, and that's the way to find out about birds. That's the way people does that writes books about birds, and loves them so that they'll go hungry and tired and take any amount of trouble to find a new bird and kill it. Their names is ornithologers, and I could have been an ornithologer myself, because I always loved birds and creatures; and I started out to learn how to be one, and I see a bird setting on a limb of a high tree, singing with its head tilted back and its mouth open and before I thought I fired, and his song stopped and he fell straight down from the limb, all limp like a rag, and I run and picked him up and he was dead, . . . and I hain't never murdered no creature since that warn't doing me no harm, and I ain't going to.

Tom Sawyer Abroad naturally invites comparison with *Huckleberry Finn*. To a considerable degree it recalls the earlier achievement in the craft of story-telling; it echoes the same easy, colloquial, accurate prose. What it lacks is the resolution of antagonistic viewpoints found in the earlier work. In *Huckleberry Finn* life on the raft is contrasted with life on shore and the superior morality of the raft community asserted. But in *Tom Sawyer Abroad* the pessimistic view dominates, even though Twain's sympathy remains the same. Huck is really no more than another example of irrational mankind, even when he expresses a sentiment with which Twain himself irrationally concurred. Huck reports Tom's rational judgment: "Whenever he heard me and Jim try to argue it made him ashamed of the human race. I never said nothing; I was feeling pretty well satisfied. . . . It's better to be generous, that's what I think." Generosity is a moral act, but a man deserves no credit for generosity if he is not responsible for his acts. Twain's implicit sympathy contradicts his explicit assertion. The same conflict also mars *Pudd'nhead Wilson*.

Ordinarily one would say little about *Pudd'nhead Wilson* and move on to other matters, content to have assigned the book a place as a minor partial success. But nearly all who have written about Twain have had good things to say about *Pudd'nhead Wilson*, and at least two critics recently have praised the book extravagantly. Leslie Fiedler says that it just fails being "the most extraordinary book in American literature . . . *Pudd'nhead Wilson* is a fantastically good book." [2] He goes on in the same vein to enlarge upon the virtues of the work. F. R. Leavis, in his introduction, calls it "the masterly work of a great writer" and "a classic in its own right." He admits that the book is not faultless, but the sum of his opinion is extremely favorable. Richard Chase, in *The American Novel and Its Tradition*, replies very well to these critics by examining the book alongside *Huckleberry Finn*. He finds that the book falls short in "that the characters and their relationships are not adequate to the moral action; the split between action and actors runs through the book." Chase is correct; if anything he is too charitable toward the flaws in the work. This kind of attention given to *Pudd'nhead Wilson* demands that we look more closely at the work.

Twain's disarming preface to *Those Extraordinary Twins* tells how he wrote himself into a dilemma when he lost sight of his original motif and the characters took over the story: ". . . it changed itself from a farce to a tragedy while I was going along with it,—a most embarrassing circumstance." His original idea that a freak as hero offered numerous possibilities for humor is evidence of his limited understanding of humor. This part was pulled out by the roots in "a kind of literary Caesarian operation," leaving what Twain called the tragedy. But *Pudd'nhead Wilson* is a tragedy only in a very broad sense; there is no character of tragic proportions in it. By the term, Twain undoubtedly meant that it was a tragedy of circumstance, for it illustrates the pessimistic ideas of his "philosophy." One cannot properly judge the work as tragedy, but rather must regard it as basically a serious story with some comic overtones.

There are really three plots. The central one concerns Roxanna, a slave nurse, who switches her own infant son with the son of her master. The deception is not discovered. Roxy's son, raised as a white boy, becomes a wastrel, and much of the plot is given over to his affairs involving theft, selling his mother, and murdering his benefactor, whose heir he is. The two secondary plots are interwoven with the main plot. One deals with Pudd'nhead Wilson chiefly as a foil for the "damned human race" aspects of the village. His interest in fingerprints provides the device by which the true identities of the two boys are ultimately revealed. The other minor plot, involving the twins, was the plot with which Twain started, but in the final version it was somewhat altered and subordinated.

Pudd'nhead Wilson is a lesser achievement than *Huckleberry Finn*. The humor in the work is of a sardonic sort, taking its tone from *Pudd'nhead Wilson's Calendar*. One redeeming feature is that Twain does finally come close to creating a satisfying full-length female character in Roxanna, probably because she was Negro and therefore could be treated as a primitive like Huck, Tom, Jim, Pap, and a lesser gallery of such characters. Not only as a character but in another way, Roxanna represents a notable achievement on Twain's part. For the first time, the institution of slavery had been dealt with relatively objectively and realistically in American fiction. Uncle Tom and Uncle Remus are childishly artificial by comparison. It is a tribute to Twain's art that the theme of miscegenation, daring in his day, was handled unobtrusively—yet without compromising the truth—and did not arouse any objection on the part of his audience. The antipathy toward the institution of slavery is generated almost incidentally to the feeling evoked by the poignant illustration of man's inhumanity to man in Roxanna's being sold down the river by her own "white" son.

The incident illustrates Twain's Calvinistic-deterministic belief that man is fundamentally evil and incapable of moral goodness. On the other hand, Roxy represents Twain's emotional desire to affirm mankind's moral responsibility, for although she later reproaches her son, she nonetheless forgives him for his despicable act. The folk mind is nothing if not charitable when one of its principles is involved: blood is thicker than water.

The book's conclusion affirms another of Twain's doctrines, that the individual is not responsible for his character, but is the product of forces outside his control. Tom Driscoll is blackhearted by the circumstances of his birth. Roxy says, "Thirty-one parts of you is white, on'y one part nigger, en dat po' little one part is yo' soul. Tain't wuth savin'; tain't wuth totin' out on a shovel en throwin' in de gutter." And in a scant paragraph Valet de 'Chambre is doomed to a life of misery because he was raised as a slave. He is free, but his conditioning as a slave haunts him the rest of his life. Twain did not see the inconsistency in this conclusion. One is damned because one thirty-second part of him was black, though he was raised as white, and the other damned because he was raised as a black, though all his ancestry was white. On one hand heredity is the factor determining character, and on the other it is environment.

In the creation of Dawson's Landing, Twain makes a worthy addition to the frontier villages he created in Obedstown and St. Petersburg. The Dauphin's observation in *Huckleberry Finn* might more appropriately have been said of Dawson's Landing: "Hain't we got all the fools in town on our side? And ain't that a big enough majority in any town?" But Twain observes the village and its inhabitants in the light of an added decade of experience. The humor has become irony, and the ironist writing *Pudd'nhead Wilson* is groping toward tragedy, which he had not defined in artistic terms. Twain returns to drawing upon his boyhood experience, but not as effectively as he had done earlier. Many of the episodes seem contrived. They seem to have been selected as evidence supporting several related theses. Again the conflict between his rational philosophy and his emotional sympathies mars the unity of the work. Roxy refutes Twain's contention about character, for she emerges as a morally responsible being who must suffer the consequences of a moral choice she made in switching the infants. And she is the most successful and convincing character in the story.

In such general matters it is not unusual to find Twain at fault. But it is surprising to find Twain remiss in matters of detail. The technical flaws in this work are somewhat more obtrusive than customary in a major work by Twain. We are accustomed to excusing his episodic structure and sometimes lame endings; these are sins of ignorance. But in *Pudd'nhead Wilson*, Twain appears to be careless in the most rudimentary aspects of the storyteller's art.

First of all, Twain was a butcher rather than a surgeon in performing his "literary Caesarian operation." In his preface to *Those Extraordinary Twins*, Twain tells us, "I took those twins apart and made two separate men of them." As normal twins Angelo and Luigi seem a curious pair. Wherever they appear in *Pudd'-nhead Wilson*, they are abnormally dependent upon one another. There is only one scene in which clearly they do not stand close together, and this is on the occasion when Luigi steps forward and kicks Tom. There are, however, several places in the book where their words and behavior are indeed puzzling for physically normal men. At the beginning of chapter VI, Angelo tells something of their history. In the course of the narrative he says, "Our parents were well to do, there in Italy, and we were their only child." And a few lines later he tells how, after the death of their parents, the twins were exhibited in a cheap museum in Berlin. In chapter XI, Wilson reads Luigi's palm and discovers that he had once killed a man. Angelo explains that Luigi had done so to protect his brother. But Luigi disclaims any heroic intention by saying, "You overlook one detail; suppose I hadn't saved Angelo's life, what would have become of mine? If I had let the man kill him wouldn't he have killed me, too? I saved my own life, you see."

Such incidents are puzzling until one learns that the twins were originally intended to be Siamese twins. Twain was simply careless in reworking his manuscript to remove these traces of his surgery. Such lapses, however, do not constitute the major flaw with respect to the twins. By his surgery Twain removed the original comic function of the twins, but he appears not to have inquired into what remaining function they performed. It is not a useful one so far as the main plot and theme are concerned. Indeed, the presence of the twins is more than just irrelevant to the central concerns of the book; their behavior is actually distracting. Their exotic personalities are a jarring note on the landscape of Dawson's Landing. The only justification would appear to be that Twain uses them satirically to point up the provincialism and gullibility of the village mentality. And Twain is not even consistent in this, for at the reception for the twins he presents the villagers as honest, simple folk, easily awed by the glamor of the occasion. Their innocence can hardly be held against them.

In his introduction to *Those Extraordinary Twins*, Twain writes of the twins: "They had no occasion to have foreign names now, but it was too much trouble to remove them all through, so I left them christened as they were and made no explanation." Of course Twain was making a joke, but like most jokes, and especially Twain's jokes, there is a large order of truth involved. The evidence suggests an unpardonable carelessness toward the construction of this tale. This tired attitude is conveyed in other ways that invite one to indict the author for not taking advantage of opportunities offered in the plot.

The character of Chambers is a case in point. He had to be invented to provide the occasion for trading places with Tom, but once invented he proved useful dramatically as a foil for Tom. And Twain makes considerable use of him in this role as the boys grow up together. The author must also have had Chambers in mind for the end of the plot, where he is unjustly accused of murder. Certainly Twain knew all this at the beginning, for the busi-

ness about the fingerprints indicates unmistakably that the trial
scene was in Twain's mind at the outset. Chambers' plight as the
white heir raised as a Negro offered a ready-made counterplot to
Tom's adventures. But what happens? After the first few chapters,
Chambers is lost, not even mentioned, until he is resurrected for
the concluding trial scene. And even there his role is only a minor
one. Twain might well have capitalized on the dramatic possibilities offered by Chambers, for he, not the twins, was really related
to the central theme of the book.

The main design of the work involves Wilson, Tom, Chambers,
and Roxy. The chapters dealing with the twins that intrude in the
body of the novel are there because Twain could not deal with
the implications of his theme adequately and was lured away on
the trail of farce instead of sticking to the exploration of his main
story. It is a promising beginning ironically treating the nature
of man's inhumanity to man—not in generalizations, but with two
specific instances. One concerns Wilson's reception by the village,
a documented case of how a man's reputation may be based upon
and fixed by a trivial incident. The other is a particularization in
the person of Roxy of the relations between Negro and white,
and it too is an ironic examination.

> To all intents and purposes Roxy was as white as anybody, but
> the one-sixteenth of her which was black outvoted the other
> fifteen parts and made her a negro. She was a slave, and salable
> as such. Her child was thirty-one parts white, and he, too, was a
> slave, and by a fiction of law and custom a negro. He had blue
> eyes and flaxen curls like his white comrade, but even the father
> of the white child was able to tell the children apart—little as he
> had commerce with them—by their clothes; for the white babe
> wore ruffled soft muslin and a coral necklace, while the other
> wore merely a coarse tow-linen shirt which barely reached to
> its knees, and no jewelry.

There is no mistaking the ironic intention, for the method is repeated a number of times throughout the second chapter. Roxy's
master discovers the theft of a small sum of money, and the slave
servants are suspected. Such petty crimes, Twain tells us, were
common and not regarded as sinful by the servants. "They had
an unfair show in the battle of life, and they held it no sin to take
military advantage of the enemy—in a small way; in a small way,

but not in a large one." When the opportunity arose, one of them might take an article of small value, "perfectly sure that in taking this trifle from the man who daily robbed him of an inestimable treasure—his liberty—he was not committing any sin that God would remember against him in the Last Great Day."

To discover the culprit, the master, Percy Driscoll, threatens the slaves with being sold. "He was a fairly humane man toward slaves and other animals; he was an exceedingly humane man toward the erring of his own race." He threatens them further that if the culprit does not confess by the end of a minute all three will be sold down the river. Immediately all three confess. The master then states that they shall be sold locally.

> The culprits flung themselves prone, in an ecstacy of gratitude, and kissed his feet, declaring that they would never forget his goodness and never cease to pray for him as long as they lived. They were sincere, for like a god he had stretched forth his mighty hand and closed the gates of hell against them. He knew, himself, that he had done a noble and gracious thing, and was privately well pleased with his magnanimity; and that night he set the incident down in his diary, so that his son might read it in after years, and thereby be moved to deeds of gentleness and humanity himself.

This ironic handling of the theme recurs in the final statement of the book, when Tom has been judged guilty of murder and imprisoned.

> Everybody granted that if 'Tom' were white and free it would be unquestionably right to punish him—it would be no loss to anybody; but to shut up a valuable slave for life—that was quite another matter.
>
> As soon as the Governor understood the case, he pardoned Tom at once, and the creditors sold him down the river.

The theme is a profoundly moving and serious one of tragic dimensions, but not as Twain handles it. Having done as much as indicated, Twain backs off and does not explore the subject further. Just as gingerly, he treats Roxy as a desirable woman, mistress of a white man, a Virginia gentleman. Saying that this was the first occasion on which the institution of slavery and miscegenation were handled relatively objectively and realistically in fiction is not the same thing as saying they were handled successfully as material for a novel. We may be grateful for what he has done and understand the reasons for his compromise, but if we judge *Pudd'nhead Wilson* fairly, we must recognize that the flawed structure of the work keeps it from being a satisfying novel.

Twain's next work, *Joan of Arc*, is a quite different book from *Pudd'nhead Wilson*, but it does continue the latter's development toward a tragic rather than a comic view of life. In many ways it is a good book, well organized, brilliantly written in several passages. But, in the final analysis, it closely follows its sources and adds nothing by way of insight to our understanding of Joan. It is rather a private book, a labor of love, and Twain knew it: "Possibly the book may not sell, but that is nothing—it was written for love." [3]

Twain was in love with Joan, and, like an adolescent, he loved without knowing much about the object of his adoration. The usual explanation has been that in Joan he found the ideal of womanhood embodying all the virtues and none of the faults of his daughter Suzy, his wife, and his "Platonic Sweetheart." Twain himself felt the symbolic power of The Maid; at the end of the book he asks the reader to accept her as the eternal symbol of patriotism.

But Joan was something much more dear to Twain, and the reason for his love is not hard to discover. In his preface he writes:

> But the character of Joan of Arc is unique. It can be measured by the standards of all times without misgiving or apprehension as to the result. Judged by any of them, judged by all of them, it is still flawless, it is still ideally perfect; it still occupies the loftiest place possible to human attainment, a loftier one than has been reached by any other mere mortal.

In Joan, Twain finds affirmation of the perfectibility of mankind. She is the lone example that history affords of an actual, real embodiment of all the virtues demonstrated by Huck and Jim and of all that he felt to be noble in man. Joan is the ideal

toward which mankind strives. Twain had to tell her story because she is the sole concrete argument against the pessimistic
doctrines of his deterministic philosophy.

Her story begins as a challenge to *Pudd'nhead Wilson*, but it
ends as a confirmation of the essentially tragic fact of human existence. Twain intended to stop at the close of Volume I with
Joan's story only half completed, but such an act would have
been an evasion. One can understand his hesitation. If it was hard
for Twain to accept the fact that even compromise with forces
of evil results in only partial achievement of man's dreams and
ideals, it must have been doubly hard for him to realize that a
failure to compromise, and faithful adherence to one's vision,
result only in total destruction.

IX

The Mysterious Stranger: Symbol and Allegory

TWAIN was no thinker, and nowhere is the essentially primitive cast of his mind more evident than in his attempts to wrestle with a problem whose scope was far beyond him. His final attempt was in the unfinished manuscript of *The Mysterious Stranger*. Bernard DeVoto regards these last years of frenzied writing as Twain's struggle to win absolution for himself. He concludes that Twain was forging symbols of despair in a frantic effort to win peace, and that he finally did so in *The Mysterious Stranger*. "The accusation begotten by experience could be stilled by destroying all experience." [1] Perhaps it was personal salvation Twain was seeking, but, if so, he was also seeking a way for his fellow man as well. In *The Mysterious Stranger* he was continuing the problem posed in *Tom Sawyer Abroad* and was trying to resolve the conflict between his sympathy for the dignity of man and his rational doctrine of man's worthlessness. The only solution he could find was the negation of reality. Life is only a dream, reality only an illusion. It is not a satisfactory solution, of course, but rather a recognition that he could not cope with the problem, for to say that a problem does not exist is not to solve it.

Twain's secretary, Albert Bigelow Paine, is said to have recognized the present ending of the story as its most fitting. Paine was not a reliable scholar nor a critic, as his biography of Twain indicates. Twain's instinct was a more trustworthy guide, and he evidently was not satisfied with the conclusion. The dream is a possible intellectual solution, but the meaning of the story in its concern with the problem of appearance and reality suggests another interpretation: that the world is a complex, fearful, frustrating, and awesome thing, not always to be understood entirely by the mind.

An intelligent examination of the book has been made by E. S. Fussell.[2] He demonstrates that in this last work Twain reached his highest achievement of structural unity; there is a coherent development to the solipsistic conclusion. The boy is led by Satan, his guide, through several instructive adventures that are half-truths necessary in order to prepare the boy for the revelation of the final truth, which in turn negates all that preceded the final revelation. But Fussell also points to the one difficulty involved in his analysis. The thematic unity he observes is undeniably present, but what, after all, can be made of the fact that Twain rejected the final chapter as an adequate conclusion? Fussell satisfactorily answers the question by pointing out that, after all, Twain did write the conclusion, whether he was happy with it or not, and we must deal with the story as we know it.

The book reflects a difference in Twain's late writing that we can get at by contrasting *The Mysterious Stranger* with his earlier work. The quality of Twain's prose had changed so greatly that it warrants a close comparison and some comment. The opening paragraphs of *The Mysterious Stranger* parallel in form the opening of *Pudd'nhead Wilson*; the beginnings follow roughly the same pattern in describing the scene of the story, but the remarkable change is in the quality of the language and choice of detail and word. The earlier work begins as follows:

> The scene of this chronicle is the town of Dawson's Landing, on the Missouri side of the Mississippi, half a day's journey, per steamboat, below St. Louis.
> In 1830 it was a snug little collection of modest one and two-story frame dwellings whose whitewashed exteriors were almost concealed from sight by climbing tangles of rose-vines, honeysuckles, and morning-glories. Each of these pretty homes had a garden in front fenced with white palings and opulently stocked with hollyhocks, marigolds, touch-me-nots, prince's feather, and other old-fashioned flowers; while on the window-sills of the houses stood wooden boxes containing moss-rose plants and terra-cotta pots in which grew a breed of geranium whose spread of

intensively red blossoms accented the prevailing pink tint of the rose-clad house-front like the explosion of flame.

The description of the town continues at some length with a wealth of specific colorful detail. Beside this example, the beginning of *The Mysterious Stranger* is drab:

> It was in 1590—winter. Austria was far away from the world, and asleep; it was still the Middle Ages in Austria, and promised to remain so forever. . . .
> Yes, Austria was far from the world, and asleep, and our village was in the middle of Austria. . . . At its front flowed the tranquil river, its surface painted with cloud-forms and the reflections of drifting arks and stone-boats; behind it rose the woody steeps to the base of the lofty precipice; from the top of the precipice frowned a vast castle, its long stretch of tower and bastions mailed in vines; beyond the river, a league to the left, was a tumbled expanse of forest-clothed hills cloven by winding gorges where the sun never penetrated; and to the right a precipice overlooked the river, and between it and the hills just spoken of lay a far-reaching plain dotted with little homesteads nested among orchards and shade trees.

Details are reduced; there is no attempt to fix concrete and specific "facts" upon the page. The effect is a blurring of detail and focusing upon the total effect of achieving a mood rather than a picture. Vividness and "seeming of reality" are partially sacrificed for a style more suggestive of a legend than a chronicle of actuality.

In a similar fashion the dialogue is not calculated to give the effect of actual speech. Indeed, the characters often make speeches rather as though they were performing on a stage. And, although Theodore Fisher is the narrator, no attempt is made to report events in the terms probable for a boy. In telling about the stranger, he uses language such as the following:

> He saw the world made; he saw Adam created; he saw Samson surge against the pillars and bring the temple down in ruins about him; he saw Caesar's death; he told of the daily life in heaven; he had seen the damned writhing in the red waves of hell; and he made us see all these things, and it was as if we were on the spot and looking at them with our own eyes. And we felt them, too, but there was no sign that they were anything to him beyond mere entertainments. Those visions of hell, those poor babes and women and girls and lads and men shrieking and supplicating in

anguish—why, we could hardly bear it, but he was as bland about it as if it had been so many imitation rats in an artificial fire.

Such rhetoric in the mouth of a young boy would be incredible if the book purported realistically to portray events, but such is not Twain's purpose.

In forging a new medium of expression, Twain had to compromise some of his earlier principles of composition. But the result is a higher degree of thematic unity and coherence than he had reached since *Huckleberry Finn* and less conflict between ideas expressed and contrary sympathies informing his style.

The reason for Twain's uncertainty about the ending is not difficult to see. The solipsism of the conclusion negates all experience. It does not exist. To one so self-conscious about his experience as Twain, the conclusion must have been repugnant, no matter how much he might subscribe to such a view rationally. Not only were his sympathies undoubtedly opposed, but also, as a logical consequence he would be forced to give up the ideas he carried next to his heart in his "bible." The latter step would have been doubly repugnant.

Twain was probably not aware of the dilemma into which he had written himself and was operating rather by intuition. But some dim awareness of the implication must have guided him in his dissatisfaction with the conclusion, in not publishing *The Mysterious Stranger* himself, and instead publishing *What Is Man?* after writing *The Mysterious Stranger*. It appears that he wrote his last novel shortly before the short story, "The Man That Corrupted Hadleyburg." The short story is by way of being an answer to the novel and explains why he did not continue with the unpublished experiments culminating in *The Mysterious Stranger*. If the dream conclusion of that book logically follows the evidence presented, then it can claim no more validity than the premises upon which it rests. The story he recounts is the minor premise, a specific instance of the major premise that the "Moral Sense" is a delusion and that man is not morally responsible for his acts. The conclusion must imply, then, that if there is no individual moral responsibility there is no meaning in life. If one rejects the conclusion, he must affirm the principle of moral obligation.

In "The Man That Corrupted Hadleyburg," the dilemma is resolved in a manner consistent with Twain's pessimistic views. While on the surface appearing to show that man is incapable of moral rectitude, Twain concludes by showing that, although man is morally weak and errant, he can be capable of moral responsibility if he constantly tests and practices it. Man is capable of goodness, but only through conscious effort in the attempt. He must not merely will to be good, but he must work at it. The conflicting views are reconciled by showing what man seems to be, as described in *What Is Man?*, and at the same stroke suggesting what man *can* become by assuming moral responsibility for himself rather than shifting the burden to a disinterested deity. In the process Twain both kept his cake and ate it, so to speak, for he could retain his pessimistic view of man's appearance and also speculate upon the possibility of differing reality. In effect he returned to his position in *Huckleberry Finn*, but far too late in his life and career; it is doubtful that he was more than dimly aware of the fact, and his novel-writing days had passed.

R. P. Blackmur calls "The Man That Corrupted Hadleyburg" a burlesque allegory. He is essentially right in defining Twain's achievement as a variety of symbolic art. So, too, is *The Mysterious Stranger* a sort of allegory, the kind that we often associate with the fairy tale. In these last pieces of fiction, Twain was near discovering the symbolic form to which his artistic struggle with reality had led him. He turns instead to the dream as a symbol, as it had been for Colonel Sellers and Tom Sawyer, a variety of fact. It is perhaps a measure of the sophistication reached by a fundamentally primitive mind that Twain moves from rendering his perception of reality in the concrete, simple prose of *Huckleberry Finn* to the more densely textured symbolism of the prose in his last years. It is also a gauge of Twain's growing sophistication that he ultimately came to the dim recognition that the only way to write more than we know, to answer unanswerable questions, to say the unsayable, is through symbols

Finally, Mark Twain is American in his art in more ways than we have allowed. This perhaps is a curious thing to say about a writer whose every page loudly announces its American origins. I have in mind, however, something more than Twain the artist much admired for the simplicity, directness, and accuracy of a supple, colloquial prose—the Twain that Hemingway meant when he said that all modern American prose that was any good came from *Huckleberry Finn*. This was the Twain that Howells called the Lincoln of our literature.

A subtler manifestation of his Americanness links him to an essentially American literary experience. Twain's is a more elemental manifestation of the same artistic progress made by such a writer as Melville. It is characteristic of these writers, and perhaps central to the classically American tradition in the novel, that they founded their art upon their firsthand experience and tried to cope with it in symbolic terms. Success came to them early, before they had fully perfected their art. One can trace in their careers the course of refining techniques from novel to novel. And this technical development parallels a course of spiritual trial, of resisting the compromises required by success, posing large questions, and tearing the answers out from the flesh of one's experience. The only help in this lonely quest is the example of the masters—those writers who have gone before.

Mark Twain followed the same course and found it a more difficult one, for he looked to no literary masters for guidance. In his miscellaneous reading he saw only examples of what not to do. Equipped with raw genius and a wealth of experience, he had to invent almost everything he knew about writing novels.

Fundamentally, Twain was a satirist before he was a novelist; and often the latter role suffered for the sake of the former. We must distinguish here between satire as a mode of expression and as a literary form. A few satirical touches make a work a satire no more than one swallow makes a drunkard. The difference is crucial for the novel, as I shall demonstrate later. Twain's *Joan of Arc*, despite an occasional satirical element, is not a satirical novel. *The Gilded Age* must be counted as a satire, but it must also be counted as a bad novel.

In the modern novel, certain technical difficulties attend the use of satire. Early satirical novelists talked directly to the reader either in extensive asides and digressions or in expository discussions. Fielding, Sterne, and Thackeray interrupted the narrative on occasion to have a little chat with the reader and tell him how to regard what was going on. More often straight expository passages from the omniscient point of view allowed the author to control the reader's attitude directly. In the satirical novel the author could establish his own persona as the controlling attitude by which the events could be judged. These conventions persisted well into the nineteenth century.

Nineteenth-century conventions in fiction, however, were moving away from such freedom in narrative point of view. Henry James's experiments resulted from pressures engendered by the rise of realism in fiction. Greater objectivity and verisimilitude were required. Twain's solution was to use humor. It was not a conscious choice, for Twain was a humorist-satirist long before he wrote a novel. Accepting the conventions of objectivity and prohibiting the author's direct statement posed no conscious problem for Twain. Humor was the satirist's most valuable weapon, according to him, and humor was his characteristic strategy in expressing a satirical attitude.

In matters of structure, however, the satirist in the novel is at a disadvantage, and Twain was no exception. The problem is that satire is poised somewhere between tragedy and comedy. In its development the novel has sought its parallels more often in comedy and tragedy than in the epic. Tragedy and comedy move toward some resolution of conflict, but in satire conflict ends where it begins. Tragedy concludes with the hero a changed man, defeated perhaps, but a wiser man; comedy finishes on an optimistic note. But no such resolution is really possible in satire, for change eliminates the cause that provokes satire. There may be action—usually a lot of it—but it all comes to no satisfactory conclusion in terms of amelioration or justice or acceptance. We may know more about the satirized subject, share the satirist's scorn, be amused or outraged, but we still end where we began, contemplating the unchanged conditions that provoked the satire.

For this reason, the most successful satirical novels of the past have been picaresque. The satirist in the novel requires some means by which a large segment of society may pass before the reader; and he requires a character, not committed deeply to the

values of a particular class or group, who can view these values
from the outside and perhaps serve as a testing intelligence. The
journey motif answers the first requirement, and the picaro the
second—the picaresque form is the most obvious and elementary
solution in narrative satire. *Huckleberry Finn* almost classically
fits the form, and time after time Twain turned again to the
picaresque, in *Tom Sawyer* and *The Prince and the Pauper* most
obviously; but indirectly in other works he structures the events
partly in picaresque form. It was, in his case, a logical extension
of his experience in his travel writing rather than a conscious
following of an established novelistic convention.

Certain limitations mark the elementary and relatively unsophisticated picaresque structure. The events in the novel are
arranged chronologically, usually with no other necessary relationship in temporal sequence. There is no inevitability in the
sequence of events that marks a more tragic plot, for example.
In addition, the protagonist must maintain his dominant attitude
consistently throughout the novel in order to sustain the satiric
tone, which places a certain restriction upon his capacity to
change in response to events. The satirist, of course, can move out
of the picaresque into other forms of the novel, but he carries
with him the technical problems of the more elementary form.

The author's problem is further complicated by his personal
response to the order and disorder of reality. In a relatively stable
society with relatively stable values, he may proceed fairly con-
fidently. But what of other times? In "A Proposal for Correcting
the English Language," Jonathan Swift says, "Satire is reckoned
the easiest of all wit, but I take it to be otherwise in very bad
times: for it is as hard to satirize well a man of distinguished vices,
as to praise well a man of distinguished virtues. It is easy enough
to do either to people of moderate characters." A small-town
jail and a hanging judge are easy targets, but not an Auschwitz
and an Eichmann. A revolution in a banana republic viewed from
a distance is easy, but what of a war with the threat of nuclear
destruction? The genial Horatian satirist avoids such large subjects. The Juvenalian satirist subordinates humor and turns to
other devices to contemplate the grotesque horror of a disordered
universe. This latter was the course Mark Twain attempted,

Twain's vision is a dark one. He is something of a pessimist and a cynic. The fretful contrast between appearance and reality, between values professed and values practiced, things as they are and things as they could be—these are his subjects. He reflects the same duality in himself. Mostly Twain takes a jaundiced view of mankind and society, but some part of him still remains optimistic enough to justify his effort, to imply that improvement is possible. Indeed, satire can exist only when there is some faith, though only implicit, in the possibility of a rational order. In *Huckleberry Finn* Twain was not very explicit about rational order, other than to imply that it resides in the common-sense view of Huck. The book is a negative examination of various facets of a particular society. The theme is one of rejection—Huck and Jim fleeing from disorder, confusion, and horror. At the conclusion Huck elects not to return to "sivilization." "I been there before," he says. Instead he speculates upon "lighting out" for the Territory. The conclusion suggests that common-sense rationality does not stand a chance in the civilized community represented by the frontier life on the Mississippi. Vaguely, however, there is hope in a new beginning on an even cruder frontier.

Some time after *Huckleberry Finn* appeared, Twain turned to the writing of *A Connecticut Yankee*. He wrote Howells that in this book he was going to have his final say on all that burned within him and longed to be expressed. It was an admission that the realistic-picaresque form of *Tom Sawyer*, *Huckleberry Finn*, and *The Prince and the Pauper* was inadequate to convey all he wished to say. In *A Connecticut Yankee* his genial humor turned to bitter wit, and fantasy provided the vehicle for his satire. It was only a partial success, and he continued to write, not solely for economic motives, but also in an attempt to find symbolic forms for the adequate expression of his ideas. These efforts culminated in *The Mysterious Stranger*. Twain had come some distance from the sunny Mississippi raft to the brooding, somber landscape of Eseldorf. He was on his way toward finding in allegory and symbolism a profounder expression of his satirical vision. The solipsistic conclusion that all is a vagrant dream is an evasion, signifying his reluctance to accept the truth of his dark view.

In matters of novelistic technique, Twain ended where many

another novelist begins. But this is understandable, for he had to discover and invent for himself practically all that he knew about the making of a novel. Twain's ordeal in his development as a novelist leads us to conclude that the satiric view of a disordered universe is likely to be a tragic vision without an adequate faith to sustain and support the viewer.

Early in his career as a novelist, Twain fortuitously put together his inventions and shaped *Huckleberry Finn,* only vaguely aware of what he had wrought. We can regret that he never really discovered the source of his myth-making power in this novel. However it was achieved, the power of this work is enough to assure Twain a secure place in the company of major American novelists, his "fellow teachers of the great public." It does not really matter that it was made by a jackleg.

Notes

Chapter I

1. W. D. Howells, *My Mark Twain* (New York, 1910), p. 6. Howells' reference is to the private life of Samuel Clemens; this study of the writer's professional life refers always to Mark Twain.
2. *Ibid.*, pp. 46-47.
3. *Ibid.*, p. 60.
4. A. B. Paine (ed.), *Mark Twain's Letters* (New York, 1924), I, 316.
5. *Harvard Library Bulletin*, IX (Spring, 1955), 164.
6. A. B. Paine, *Mark Twain, A Biography* (New York, 1912), p. 607.
7. *Ibid.*, pp. 607-8.
8. *Ibid.*, pp. 608-9.
9. Paine (ed.), *Letters*, I, 317-18.
10. *Ibid.*, II, 374.
11. Cyril Clemens, *Mark Twain, The Letter Writer* (Boston, 1932), p. 25.
12. Paine (ed.), *Letters*, II, 527.
13. Howells, *My Mark Twain*, pp. 143-44.
14. Bernard DeVoto, *Mark Twain's America* (Boston, 1932), p. 302.
15. J. H. Randall, *The Making of the Modern Mind* (New York, 1940), p. 31

Chapter II

1. Stephen B. Leacock, *Humor and Humanity* (New York, 1933), pp. 218-19.
2. Bernard DeVoto (ed.), *Mark Twain in Eruption* (New York, 1940), p. 202.
3. Mark Twain, *Works* (Author's National Edition), XXII, 11.
4. Leacock, *Humor and Humanity*, p. 219.
5. Paine (ed.), *Letters*, I, 223.
6. George Bainton (ed.), *The Art of Authorship* (New York, 1890).
7. Paine (ed.), *Letters*, II, 421-22.
8. Dixon Wecter (ed.), *The Love Letters of Mark Twain* (New York, 1949), p. 227.

9. A. B. Paine (ed.), *Mark Twain's Notebook* (New York, 1935), p. 192.

10. A. B. Paine (ed.), *Mark Twain's Speeches* (New York, 1910), p. 389.

11. Mark Twain, *Following the Equator*, ch. XV.

12. A. B. Paine (ed.), *Mark Twain's Autobiography* (New York, 1924), I, 92-93, 174.

Chapter III

1. Dixon Wecter (ed.), *Mark Twain to Mrs. Fairbanks* (San Marino, Cal., 1949), p. 171.

2. Paine, *Biography*, p. 8.

3. Paine (ed.), *Autobiography*, I, 88.

4. Paine, *Biography*, p. 68.

5. Paine (ed.), *Autobiography*, I, 88-94.

6. *Ibid.*, I, 89.

7. Twain, *Following the Equator*, ch. V.

Chapter IV

1. DeVoto (ed.), *Twain in Eruption*, pp. 262-63.

2. Paine (ed.), *Letters*, II, 345.

3. *Ibid.*, I, 309.

4. Paine (ed.), *Speeches*, p. 99.

5. Wecter (ed.), *Twain to Mrs. Fairbanks*, p. 196.

6. Wecter (ed.), *Love Letters*, p. 227.

7. Paine (ed.), *Letters*, II, 563.

8. *Ibid.*, I, 266.

9. Mark Twain, *What Is Man? and Other Essays* (New York, 1917), p. 229.

10. Mark Twain, *A Connecticut Yankee in King Arthur's Court*, ch. CV.

11. Mark Twain, *A Tramp Abroad*, appendix.

12. Twain, *A Connecticut Yankee*, ch. XXV.

13. Mark Twain, *Europe and Elsewhere*, ed. A. B. Paine (New York and London, 1923), p. 341.

14. Opie P. Read, *Mark Twain and I* (Chicago, 1940), p. 38.

15. Paine (ed.), *Letters*, I, 227.

16. Brander Matthews, *The Tocsin of Revolt and Other Essays* (New York, 1922), pp. 265-66.

17. Paine (ed.), *Letters*, I, 258.

18. *Ibid.*, I, 271.

19. *Ibid.*, I, 258.

20. *Ibid.*, I, 267.

21. *Ibid.*, I, 272.
22. *Ibid.*
23. *Ibid.*, II, 477.
24. *Ibid.*, I, 224.

Chapter V

1. Paine (ed.), *Letters*, I, 243.
2. Paine (ed.), *Autobiography*, I, 237.
3. Mark Twain, *Roughing It*, ch. VIII.
4. Mark Twain, *Pudd'nhead Wilson*, pp. 115-16.

Chapter VI

1. De Lancey Ferguson, *Mark Twain: Man and Legend* (Indianapolis, Ind., 1943), p. 201.
2. Paine (ed.), *Letters*, II, 377.
3. *Ibid.*, II, 514.
4. Paine, *Biography*, pp. 887-88.

Chapter VII

1. Paine, *Biography*, ch. XVI.
2. Paine (ed.), *Notebook*, p. 81.
3. *Ibid.*, p. 395.
4. Paine (ed.), *Letters*, I, 40.
5. Paine, *Biography*, p. 411.
6. *Ibid.*, pp. 412-13.
7. *Ibid.*, p. 1583.
8. Paine (ed.), *Notebook*, p. 344.
9. Twain, *Europe and Elsewhere*, p. 406.
10. Paine (ed.), *Notebook*, p. 345.
11. Yvor Winters, *In Defense of Reason* (New York, 1939), p. 9.
12. Mark Twain, "The Turning Point in My Life," *Harper's Bazaar*, XIV (February, 1910), 118-19.
13. Paine (ed.), *Notebook*, p. 385.
14. Paine, *Biography*, p. 99.
15. *Ibid.*, p. 103.
16. *Ibid.*, p. 744.
17. Paine (ed.), *Letters*, II, 785.
18. *Ibid.*, II, 769.
19. *Ibid.*, II, 703.
20. *Ibid.*, II, 769-70.
21. Paine (ed.), *Notebook*, p. 347.
22. Twain, *What Is Man?*, p. 102.

23. Paine (ed.), *Speeches*, p. 30.
24. Paine (ed.), *Notebook*, p. 210.
25. Paine, *Biography*, p. 1583.
26. *Ibid.*, p. 1357.
27. DeVoto (ed.), *Twain in Eruption*, p. 316.
28. Paine (ed.), *Speeches*, p. 276.
29. Paine (ed.), *Notebook*, p. 237.
30. DeVoto (ed.), *Twain in Eruption*, p. 316.
31. Twain, *A Tramp Abroad*, ch. XVIII.

Chapter VIII

1. Van Wyck Brooks, *The Ordeal of Mark Twain* (New York, 1920), p. 146.
2. Leslie A. Fiedler, "As Free as Any Cretur. . . ," *New Republic*, CXXXIII (Aug. 15, 1955), 17.
3. Paine (ed.), *Letters*, II, 624.

Chapter IX

1. Bernard DeVoto, *Mark Twain at Work* (Cambridge, Mass., 1942), p. 130.
2. E. S. Fussell, "The Structural Problem of *The Mysterious Stranger*," *Studies in Philology*, XLIX (1952), pp. 95-104.

Index